Not at the Table, Please!

Quirico S. Samonte, Jr.

Illustrated by
Judith E. Samonte

FERNE PRESS

Samonte, Quirico S., Jr.
Summary: The author shares stories of adolescent mischief, growing up in the Philippines, and cross-cultural experiences in his career both in the United States and abroad.

ISBN: 978-1-933916-03-3
I. Samonte, Quirico S., Jr. II. Not at the Table, Please!
I. Family. II. Coming of age. III. Philippines. IV. Ilocos Norte. V. Cross-cultural experiences.

Library of Congress Control Number: 2006937222

FERNE PRESS

Ferne Press is an imprint of Nelson Publishing & Marketing
366 Welch Road, Northville, MI 48167
www.nelsonpublishingandmarketing.com
(248) 735-0418

Dedication

These recollections are dedicated to my spirited contemporaries of younger days, especially classmates from Class 1948 of the Ilocos Norte Provincial High School as it was then called, who never forgot their role as responsible adult citizens when they took their place in society.

Acknowledgement

I t was fun reliving the following stories as I wrote them. It was not so easy, however, to determine the boundaries of my narration. I was cognizant, for example, of the need to exercise discretion and not to give the wrong impression about what kids can do. Toward this end, a number of relatives and friends have been very helpful and encouraging. I am grateful to my sister Astrid Samonte Gorospe and my cousins Anita Samonte Jencks, Ruth Samonte Limjuco, and Virgilio "Bingo" Samonte, who took the time to read the manuscript. Although some of them commented in jest that the stories were "not steamy enough," they helped in verifying some of my recollections and also in giving me that extra measure of confidence that the materials would certainly pass the censorship of the more prudish members of our family.

Adelwisa Agas Weller, University of Michigan Lecturer in Philippine languages and culture, and Gloria Lorenzana Agas, my friends from the Ilocos region of the Philippines, have again been very helpful in checking that my Ilocano terms were not archaic. It was equally constructive for them to alert me to the possibility that some readers who are not familiar with our culture in the "North" (the Ilocano-speaking region of Luzon in the Philippines) may not appreciate the significance and humor of some of the stories; hence, more background material would be helpful. Aside from being pleasant to work with, Sarah Hart and Ryan Schrauben of Ferne Press have been very thorough and constructive as editors.

I am pleased, too, that my grandson, Brooklyn, has been able to contribute again to the illustrations. In a sense, his contribution maintains his connection to my effort to record memories that are really a part of his legacy.

My wife, Judy, who has been able to review the materials from the perspectives of a native-born American and of one now thoroughly familiar with some of my stories, has provided that essential balance that would help the narrations transcend boundaries between our two cultures. Her careful editing and humorous illustrations have amplified and injected more life into the stories.

Table of Contents

Part IV - Travel

Part V - Epilogue

Introduction

When I asked my cousin "Bingo" to review the draft of my previous book, *At the Table with the Family*, I was a bit amused when, somewhat teasingly, he said, "I wish the materials included your other exciting adventures in Laoag when you were a young man." After giving some thought to his comment, I had to concede eventually that in order to balance my recollections about growing up in Laoag, I should include a few selections that I would have refrained from telling in front of our elders or in polite company. Thus, the title of this book, *Not at the Table, Please!*

The following stories are not intended for the squeamish or those who have been shielded from the rough but sometimes seductive edges of society. A few of these recollections represent, nonetheless, the choices available to young boys growing up in the province, especially those who had that "vision thing": the courage or stubbornness to push beyond the limits of what the elders allowed; those who were maturing to become more aware of the attractions and complexities of the opposite sex; and those who were more inclined to subscribe to the pleasure principle and, therefore, prone to take reckless chances to amuse themselves and/or torment others.

Lest I give the impression of preparing you, the reader, for confessions about wanton debauchery or lawlessness, I should set you straight right away. In retrospect, our shenanigans in the 1930s in Laoag were relatively benign and harmless compared to what we read in the papers nowadays such as binge drinking, drugs, group sex, rapes, violence, runaways, etc. But from the perspective of a pre-industrial, traditional, and relatively homogeneous society, minor infractions of established norms still provided a youthful sense of recklessness and adventure. I am sure our local people did not suffer from any sense of moral degradation when, for example, a chicken for *arroz caldo* (thick rice and chicken soup) or a goat for *caldereta* (goat stew) went missing, appropriated as it were from the respective homes of the participants for an evening of camaraderie in the neighborhood. Scolding, even when muted so the neighbors would not hear about it, was taken more seriously when it was provoked, for instance, by one's overly friendly situation with one of the maids. Enough of that before I get ahead of myself.

This collection of stories is not exclusively autobiographical. It also includes narrations I heard while I was growing up. Inclusion of other sources is intended to show the extent and range of possible temptations, delights, and challenges that attended coming of age in Laoag. I have also included some adventures in connection with my assignments abroad.

I have sometimes speculated how my decision to stay in the United States after the completion of my graduate program altered the possibilities in my professional life. Nonetheless, I am grateful to the University of the Philippines for the scholarship that enabled me to pursue my graduate studies at the University of Michigan. Additionally, the University of the Philippines allowed me to reimburse the scholarship "plus interest" as a means of fulfilling the terms of my contract instead of returning to the Philippines. Thus, having maintained a good relationship with the university, I always make it a point to visit my alma mater whenever I am in the Philippines. I was even invited to teach at the university during one of my visits.

Given some of the "wilder" aspects of our upbringing in the province of Ilocos Norte, did we grow up more avaricious, less morally upright, less concerned about issues of social justice, and less ambitious than those brought up with the conveniences of modern technology, better nutrition, and no shortage of "expert" ideas about child rearing? I have my opinions, but then that should be for other people, and posterity, to judge.

Part I

More Memories
Growing Up

Agkitang

The Laoag River was a narrow, clear, and gentle ribbon of water that flowed from the Cordilleras in the east to the China Sea in the west from November through April. That period coincided approximately with our dry season in the province of Ilocos Norte. A larger area of the wide riverbed was dry at that time of the year. Portions close to the water were quite fertile and were cultivated by people who grew beans, corn, tomatoes, peanuts, sweet potatoes, and other vegetables. The rest of the dry riverbed was sandy and empty except at night when kids played in the moonlight, and when lovers met hoping for a cover of darkness.

During the dry season, the river became an artery hosting such activities as washing clothes, bathing and watering of work animals, swimming, fishing, and harvesting piles of small branches, called *rama,* which were then used as habitat to lure fish, shrimps, small crabs, and sometimes eels. The harvest of a *rama* was usually an occasion for a family picnic for the owners.

For boys out of school during the long summer vacation, swimming and picnics, even with just a watermelon or with fruits sometimes picked from somebody's backyard, were always fun. More exciting, since it involved a bit of stealth, skill, and danger, was "visiting" somebody's *kitang. Agkitang*, an *Ilocano* verb derived from the root *kitang,* was a form of fishing in which a number of baited hooks were suspended at regular intervals from a long line that floated down the river. There could be as many as twenty or more hooks, and one end of the main line was tied to a bamboo peg pounded into the sandy river bottom. A few inches of the peg stuck above the water surface as a marker, and one could tell it was for a *kitang* because a little bit of line was visible. The rest was immersed in the shallower part of the flowing water.

For kids looking for adventure and mischief, checking somebody's *kitang* was irresistible. It usually belonged to a fisherman who might be taking a nap on shore under a crudely fashioned lean-to of bamboo pegs and coconut or banana leaves. After verifying the placement of the anchor peg and the location of the napping fisherman, we determined where to take off our clothes and where to hide them. A plan for a quick getaway was essential and usually involved putting our clothes away from the fisherman, preferably on the opposite bank of the river.

The next step was to decide on a strategy. The usual approach was to float down towards the peg while hiding from one *rama* to another. Essential to the success of this scheme was being quiet, keeping a very low profile with just a part of the head above water, and moving slowly down with the current to simulate a floating coconut. Still, there were no guarantees that the man under the lean-to was not watching us the entire time as we plotted and refined our plan.

We would submerge as we got closer to the anchor peg. By holding the line under water, one could easily tell if there was a tug further down, a sure sign of a catch! Lucky days yielded us quite a bit of fish, all of it directly depriving the napping fisherman who might at the very moment be dreaming about a pot of hot *sinigang* (simmered fish with herbs and spices), *tinuno* (grilled fish), *linengta* (steamed), *ginisar* (fried) or just *kinilaw* (raw fish or shrimp with vinegar and spiced with ginger, tomatoes, and hot pepper). However mouth-watering these dishes were, I never took our catch home. My folks would not have allowed it; I had no doubts about that! My companions in these adventures, my friends from another section of the neighborhood, gladly took them home. Anyway, it would be another fun-filled summer day for me and I would arrive home with a huge appetite for whatever meal awaited me.

Less lucky days might involve a suddenly awakened fisherman waving a stick at us and shouting colorful expletives. We would scamper out of the water in our birthday suits, run to our clothes, and hastily retreat while hanging on to our catch, if we had any. Our clothes were wadded under one arm while we ran. We did not dare take the time to put them on until we were far enough from the irate fisherman!

There are stories about this form of fishing other than those of kids taking advantage of fishermen prone to taking a nap. *Tio* Salio (Rosalio Segundo, a younger brother of Mother) recalls the following in his letter (April 3, 2004):

An angry fisherman

This *"Agkitang"* chapter reminds me of what happened to me and my younger brother, Ating [Nicolas Segundo, Jr.], when we joined Nariong to *agkitang* in Sta. Maria [a barrio outside Laoag]. He tied the *kitang* near the edge for Ating and me, and he put one for him in a deeper part of the river. We caught a lot of *bocto* [small fish like smelts]. Our small *alat* [fish basket made of bamboo] was filled to the brim. Unfortunately, because of our excitement and the strong current of the river, our *alat* was carried away by the current without us noticing it.

When we informed Nariong about it, he did not say anything, but we could tell how dismayed he was from his expression. Notwithstanding the loss of our catch, his big *alat* was full of big *boctos* and we were very happy. In spite of our carelessness, he divided his catch into two parts and gave us the other half, probably because the *caratela* which brought us to the river was ours.

Some of us were fortunate indeed to grow up close to a beautiful river that provided many happy memories of family picnics, rendezvous for lovers along the riverside, learning how to swim, and the excitement as kids trying to outwit the fishermen. But we were constantly reminded by our elders to be aware of the dangers that attended such activities. For those careful enough to observe the reasonable limits of what we could safely do, the various riverside activities provided not only fun and excitement, but also valuable lessons in survival.

Baket Lucía

How can I ever forget my journeys into the spirit world with Lola Sabina! Grandchildren would sit on the *basar* (bamboo floor) around her in the evening to listen to her stories about creation, courage, and loyalty. But I think what we liked best were those scary ones about the *kapri* or *pugot* (the dark one)*, aswang* (half human, half animal)*, or *sinan padi* (like a priest). When she started her narrations about these malevolent spirits, we crowded closer around her. We did not want to take any chances.

Stories about the spirit world abound, an almost endless source of entertainment for children in different parts of the Philippines. The storyteller would modify the circumstances to fit the local setting. As Raymundo S. Punongbayan notes:

> The Philippines is a country rich in legends and myths, in what may be called the "gossip network" of its history. Place names, the creation of mountains, the origin of plants and rivers, the causes behind the eruption of volcanoes, all have their stories. The

9

number of myths about the country's natural features is not at all surprising, given the variety of its land forms. (*Kasasayan*, p. 11)

Punongbayan writes about *Manaul*, a bird in flight that found no place to stop. It implored *Kaptan*, the god of the sea, and *Magauayan*, the god of the air, to provide a place to rest. The ensuing battle between the two competing gods resulted in the formation of the first land where *Manaul* finally could rest. Another story cited by Punongbayan is about Bernardo Carpio who is forever chained between two mountains to keep them from colliding with each other. It is when Carpio pauses to rest, the legend goes, that we have an earthquake.

Luis Francia, in his interesting book, *Eye of the Fish* (2001), recalls:

> And isn't a part of childhood's essence the ambivalence towards Nature? No one feels the creative-destructive, the Brahma/Kali, forces of the world more vividly, more vibrantly, than a child. While on Siquijor, I felt that childhood uneasiness again: the night as repository of wild imaginings, the thick knots of trees as havens for ghostly creatures as the *kapre,* a cheroot-smoking ogre with unnaturally long legs; the *tikbalang,* half human, half horse; and the *manananggal,* a fetus-sucking female vampire that would leave her lower half in some hidden spot while the upper half flew in search of a pregnant woman. These monsters assumed once again an easy familiarity in my head, tap-dancing on my brain, and becoming part of a fairy-tale landscape. (Francia, p. 224)

Back to Laoag. Although *Lola* Sabina's narrations about spirits were always entertaining, some of her stories were probably intended to inculcate a bit of discipline in us young ones. For example, we were not to throw stones at the trees or else we might hit some unseen spirits like the *kapri* or *pugot* and unleash upon ourselves dreadful consequences; and we were not to play in the woods at noon when people should be taking their nap, in case we unknowingly offended the *aswang* lurking therein. These warnings definitely made me think twice before venturing into the woods on my own! And the fact that some adults seemed to believe in these stories gave them weight in my mind.

As recalled in my other book, *At the Table with the Family*, some evenings *Lola* Sabina would visit the neighborhood *basi* (sugar cane wine) store for a drink. She could buy wine by the glass for two centavos, equivalent to one cent in US currency in the 1930s. She and three or four other friends would sit on bamboo benches under an awning extending from the front door of the house of *Baket* Anneng, the *basi* vendor. We sometimes accompanied *Lola* to her watering hole for there were always entertaining stories, especially when those drinkers tried to outdo each other with tales about their "encounters" with the spirits that were supposed to inhabit old trees and abandoned buildings. The more *basi* they consumed, the more exciting their stories became! These sessions sometimes lasted into late hours. They would then part company merrily and walk home in various directions.

One evening, having had her nightcap of *basi, Baket* Lucia, one of Lola's drinking friends, was on her way home. She was never too confident walking alone late at night under the huge tamarind tree by the old Samonte house. But that was the short way, just two blocks to her *nipa* hut which she shared with her dog. She usually sang after she drank a little too much, and

Waiting for *Baket* Lucia

would keep up her singing as she approached the tamarind tree. It must have been her way of bolstering her courage as she walked alone in the dark.

It was when *Baket* Lucia was under the tamarind tree, that particular night, that something came crashing down with a loud nerve-shattering noise right behind her. *Baket* Lucia screamed. Without looking back, she took off as fast as her skinny old legs could carry her. Her *tingol* (hair bun) was undone, but she prudently chose to hang on to her *dwa na-ig* (sarong) even as it started to unwind when she dashed like a scared cat. Dogs started barking, and windows opened as people looked out to see what the commotion was all about.

The following evening at *Baket* Anneng's, *Baket* Lucia was the center of attention as she recalled her close call with the *sinan padi,* that she reaffirmed "inhabited that tamarind tree." This was embellished with her description of what "he" looked like. My cousin Erning and I huddled closer to *Lola* Sabina and listened.

Conversation at the table with the Samonte family centered also on the disturbance in the neighborhood the previous night. If only our elders had asked Erning and me if we knew anything, but that would never have happened. Children, as commonly expected at that time in Laoag, were to be seen, not heard. Erning and I concentrated quietly on the *igado* (spiced meat dish of pork liver and loin) and on the *pinakbet* (vegetable stew with eggplant as the main ingredient).

Truth to be told, Erning and I, who were then in the elementary grades, had suspended from the tamarind tree an old bucket filled with empty cans and some stones for added weight and velocity. Erning, as soon as I gave him the signal,

A *sinan padi* "descends" behind *Baket* Lucia

13

released the other end of the suspension rope that ran from the pail over the tamarind branch all the way to the base of one of *Mama* Ti's *chico* trees. With *Baket* Lucia singing as she approached the tamarind tree, it was easy for me to determine the exact time for Erning to let go his end of the rope so the bucket would land behind *Baket* Lucia, not in front of her or on her head! What a glorious night that was for Erning and me, and it probably stimulated more stories for years about the "haunted" tamarind tree by the old Samonte house.

The Revenge of
Baket Lucia

Sunshine, rain, and tropical temperatures nourished a variety of fruit trees that yielded a rich harvest every year in our old neigborhood in Laoag. I fondly remember the colors and fragrance of ripe guavas, oranges, *anangka* (jack fruit), *atis* (sugar apple), papaya, mangoes, *sarguelas* (Spanish plum), *salamagi* (tamarind), *longboy* (Java plum), *caimito* (star apple), and *guayabano* (soursop), just to name a few. While some fruits were seasonal, others fruits were borne year-round. And since each house had one or more trees, there was variety even within a relatively small area.

The children could tell when the plants flowered, and took note of the appearance later of little fruits that finally matured into plump and juicy wonders of nature. When this happened, timing was important. The *panniki* (fruit bats) seemed to know that, too, for that is when they flew in at night in search of their favorite snack. In the evening after we were all tucked in for the night, we could hear those nocturnal creatures as they noisily competed for the harvest. On moonlit nights when we were allowed to play outside, we could see their long wingspan when they approached a tree, and the branches would bend and sway as the hungry bats descended and found a foothold.

We watched out, too, for things that could easily escape the naked eye. I avoided over-ripe fruits for I could not stand those tiny wriggly maggots that reminded me of creatures that slither. Less threatening were the ripe mangoes *nga nagbortong* (that had spots in the flesh) which some folks attributed to *na-arbisan* (untimely showers).

Keeping track of the owners of a particular tree that was getting ready for picking was another matter. The owners were probably aware of the bats, too, for that meant the fruits were getting ripe. But we also had to assume that the bats were not their only worry. They must have suspected the kids in the neighborhood had as much appetite as the *panniki*. So we avoided, when we were in their vicinity, making eye contact with the owners of a particular tree that was ready for picking.

People in the neighborhood knew which lot had a particularly sweet variety of whatever was in season. For example, *Baket* Lucia, who lived by herself with her large dog, had the sweetest *salamagi* in the neighborhood. The children kept track of that tree; so did some of the pregnant women who yearned to eat something from the fruit trees that were in season. This phenomenon of craving, which occurred during early pregnancy, was referred to as *pinaginaw* by the older folks

Siesta time would not work for us as far as *Baket* Lucia's *salamagi* was concerned. Even if she was taking a nap, or sleeping off a heavy night at *Baket* Anneng's *basi* store, she was sure to be awakened by her dog's barking. So we took note of the time she went to the river to wash clothes, for she would be away for at least an hour or two. It was easy to tell if she was going to do her laundry for she carried the bundle on her head, and her *malo* (small wooden paddle for washing clothes) and a small *palang-gana* (basin) with one hand. It was not just the washing that took time. The freshly washed clothes were later spread on the hot stones to dry. Even more time-consuming was the process of washing some white clothes with a little bit of *anyel* (blue tint); after spreading them on the hot stones she occasionally poured river water on them with her *palang-gana.* This made the whites whiter. If *Baket* Lucia was preparing for a special occasion like going to a wake or a funeral, she might even bring her ingredients for a *golgol* (shampoo) which would include a piece of *lipay* (fragrant bark) and some *cab-orao* (a variety of lemon). With water in her *palang-gana*, she squeezed the bark after soaking it, and then added the *caborao* juice. Incidentally, when mother washed my hair at home with that similar mixture, I remember it was somewhat slippery but had a pleasant lemony fragrance. Once in a while *Baket* Lucia brought her dog along for a bath. But even when the dog was left behind at her *nipa* hut, his barking was obviously no longer an impediment to the adventurous and calculating kids of the neighborhood.

One time when *Baket* Lucia went to the river, two playmates and I were alerted to the opportunity and we wasted no time. Her *nipa* hut was a block away from my grandparents' house, and it was in an unfenced lot. So it was no problem walking right up to the tree. It was at least fifty feet in height and about two feet in diameter at the trunk. It had a lot of branches that spread out, and the lower limbs drooped close to the ground. Its branches were strong and flexible, a good climbing tree altogether. We were soon up there enjoying the sweetest *salamagi* in the neighborhood.

After what must have been an hour, *Baket* Lucia came back unexpectedly. With our chattering, she apparently knew right away there were boys up in her tree. She shouted at us to come down at once. As long as we remained high up in the tree, however, we knew there was nothing she could really do. So we stayed put, and continued our harvest. That must have incensed her to no end. She started throwing invectives at us. *"Sapay koma ta agsakit ta boksit yo."* ("May your stomach ache.") As if that was not enough, she added, *"Sapay koma ta ag-gongap kayo."* ("May you end up with twisted mouth!") When she realized that her verbal salvos were not getting anywhere, she brought out her dog and tied it at the base of the tree! We sat up there in our airy perches wondering what to do.

Eventually it became that time of the day for *Baket* Lucia to visit *Baket* Anneng's *basi*. Seemingly secure in the thought that she had us "treed," off she went for her costumary *sokmon* (nip of *basi*). At first, none of us dared descend and confront the dog. But after we calculated that the rope tied to the dog extended probably no more than five feet from the base of the tree, we figured our way out safely from *Baket* Lucia's contraption. The three of us climbed down, and maneuvered to the extended branches close to the ground, away from the base of the tree, and beyond the reach of the dog. Back safely on the ground and with our shirts filled with *salamagi*, we walked home satiated and victorious. Meanwhile, *Baket* Lucia was probably enjoying her *basi* at *Baket* Anneng's, savoring the thought that she had finally "fixed" those *salamagi*-eating monkeys!

Barbero

The other day I went to my favorite barber in Ann Arbor. It had been almost a month since I had had a haircut, and "angel wings" were beginning to sprout. Judy sometimes says they look nice as they curl up a little bit. I look at my hair differently, however, when I think it is growing too long. I do not want to be regarded as one of those aging campus fixtures who, for whatever reason, grow their thinning hair so they can have an under-nourished-looking rat tail. I do not know if that hairstyle is the effect of living in a university town, a setting that sometimes appears to attract and/or breed eccentrics and style freaks.

In Ann Arbor, 2006, I pay eighteen dollars for a haircut that takes just twenty minutes to complete, no razor to trim the sideburns and the back, no shaving lotion to give you that nice stinging sensation, and no massage. And the haircut is finished even faster if there are other customers waiting. I wonder what this world is coming to. Maybe there is a sensible reason for the rat tail after all! Anyway, that got me thinking about the "good old days." Yes, there were such days in Laoag when I could really get a decent haircut for free, or just a single cigarette for the barber! It got more expensive when I was in high school in the 1940s, the time when I started going to a regular barbershop. I paid ten *centavos* which was equivalent to five American cents based on the rate of exchange of two Philippine pesos to one US dollar.

When I was still of preschool age, Father usually cut my hair. He brought a chair to the garden, added a *bangkito* (small wooden stool) to increase my elevation, and draped a *dwa na-ig* (sarong) over my shoulders to keep the hair from my clothes. Haircut by Father was an event I never looked forward to for it seemed to last for an hour, much too long for me. The cloth that he draped over my shoulders made me hot and sweaty. Some of the hair that was trimmed stuck to my skin, and that was itchy. It was a relief, therefore, by the time I was in the upper elementary grades to have my hair cut by the young men in the neighborhood. They did it more quickly than Father. There was *Mang* Ben or *Mang* Carmelo, both high school students at that time, and they charged only five centavos. But I had to put up with their dull razor that tended to pull the hair, and that was painful. If it was not raining they brought out a chair or an over-turned *alsong* (large wooden mortar) for me to sit on under a tree where it was shady and cooler. I also learned how to cut hair later on, and that came in handy because the older boys in the neighborhood could trim each other's hair for free.

How did we ever learn to cut hair? There were always lots of kids around and, in the squatter's section of the neighborhood, their parents were only too glad to have us practice on their children! Earlier efforts produced results that looked a bit like the rice terraces (*ticap-ticap*), but the parents just chuckled, and eventually our skills improved.

Returning to Manila for a visit one summer in the 1980s, I mentioned to Father that I was going out for a haircut. He said, "You do not have to." Not again, I thought, since I was reminded of our hair-cutting sessions a long time ago. Before I could come up with a good excuse, he said the barber could come to the house. Yes, a barber on house call, and it did not take him long to show up at the house. I had my hair cut in style: in the garden, complete with shaving lotion, and ending with a massage of the neck and shoulders. A job well done indeed! He charged me twenty *pesos*, and I gave a ten-peso tip! At an exchange rate of fifty Philippine pesos to a US dollar at that time, no wonder American businesses are outsourcing many jobs from the United States to developing countries.

Caldereta

I remember a colleague, while I was working overseas, who occasionally invited some of his friends for dinner. He liked to serve his version of ethnic recipes, and apparently took pride in identifying for his guests the countries the food represented. While such dinners should have been occasions for culinary adventure, his cooking was, unfortunately, not always recognizable in terms of the culture or sub-culture it was supposed to represent. But it was always a good time for companionship, and we were more forgiving as the wine flowed generously.

I try a little cooking at home now and then. Being a bit leery about preparing cuisine from other lands, I tend to rely mainly on my recollections of simple, regional, peasant, and even street-corner versions of a few selected recipes from the Philippines. These include, for example, local versions of *arroz caldo* (thick rice chicken soup), *pancit* (noodles), *sinuman* (sticky rice cooked in sweetened coconut cream), and a variety of *kilawen* (goat meat, fresh fish, or shrimp eaten rare or raw with spices), *tinuno* (grilled) or *linengta* (boiled or steamed) vegetables, poultry, fish, pork, or beef.

For some of the young boys growing up in Laoag, learning to prepare these simple recipes was a time for camaraderie when we had occasional cookouts while camping or at somebody's house when the elders were away. The more spartan the setting, the more fun and enjoyable it was. Thus, we learned some culinary secrets and skills from each other. Stories from our fathers added to our repertoire, not to mention learning how resourceful they were as young boys in producing ingredients they needed for their party.

Father recalled one cookout in Laoag with some of his high school friends in the neighborhood. It was a special night since the main course was *caldereta* (goat stew), accompanied with all the extras like *kilawen*, and other kinds of *pulutan* (snack usually washed down with alcoholic drinks). When Father was getting ready to leave the house for the evening out, Uncle Vicente, his older brother, asked if he could go with Father. The two of them joined the rest of their friends at the designated location. Cooking of the *caldereta* was underway, and the other boys were already enjoying the *pulutan* of *tinuno* and *kilawen*. Father and Uncle Vicente joined a night of good food, entertaining stories, and warm companionship. Towards the end of all that merriment, as a Filipino-American old-timer in Chicago later recalled, Uncle Vicente requested all those present to be on the lookout for "one of the goats of *Tata* [Father] that has been missing!" Everybody, after a moment of silence, solemnly assured Uncle Vicente that they would be on the lookout for that goat. I wonder if Uncle Vicente, who helped demolish the *kilawen, tinuno,* and *caldereta,* ever found out that *Lolo* Justo's missing goat had been Father's contribution to the evening meal.

"One of the goats of Tata has been missing."

Private Enterprise

I cannot forget the enterprising kids in our neighborhood in Laoag who made use of fruits or other crops in season to earn money. They prepared *inartem* (pickled) green mangoes, green papaya, or *balayang* (banana with seeds). Although I had reservation about how sanitary the pickles were, I could usually rely on the corn, sweet potato, or *dip-pig* (cooking banana), which the children prepared as *linengta* (boiled) or *tinuno* (grilled). These items, pickled, boiled, or grilled, sold quickly to other customers. Consequently, when they set up their table near a *sari sari* store (small neighborhood shop) to take advantage of the traffic, the elderly woman running the *sari sari* store did not appreciate the competition at all. All she could do, however, was grumble.

Some children in the Philippines have to learn early to fend for themselves. They have to be quick on their feet in order to survive—sometimes literally, such as the cigarette and chewing gum vendors in Manila who have to run and weave between the traffic to sell their goods. Other resourceful kids sell trinkets, cards, prayer books, or bottled water for medicine in some religious sites. On one of my visits to a town outside Manila, four or five kids with religious items for sale quickly surrounded me. They kept saying, "Buy a gift for the wife, Sir. Buy a gift for the wife, Sir." In an effort to discourage one persistent girl after the other vendors left, I said jokingly that I was a Moslem. We were at that time in a Roman Catholic setting. To further complicate matters, I told the young girl, who was probably no more than ten years old, that I had four wives! That should fix her, I thought. Without missing a beat, she looked me straight in the eye and responded. "Then buy four, Sir!" I bought four *stampitas* (religious cards) that I distributed to the maids when I got home!

Back home, my youngest sister, Amy, who was then in junior high school, also had some ideas about making money. She came home one day with a couple of her girl friends and announced to Mother that they had thought of a plan to make money. Mother was pleased, and she asked what they had in mind. They said they were going to bake some cookies and sell them in the neighborhood. Amy added they might even take orders for bigger items like cake or *binbingka* (local cake sometimes made out of gelatinous rice). But could they use Mother's kitchen? Of course, said Mother.

They baked their cookies, while Mother attended to her sewing. Amy and her friends packaged the cookies nicely on paper plates and went from one house to another around the neighborhood. It did not take them long to sell the cookies. They came back excited and divided the money among themselves. They asked Mother if they could do it again the following week. Mother was pleased and encouraged them with their enterprise. After the second week, Mother was amused when she discovered that the young bakers had used up her supply of flour and sugar!

Mother scheduled a little conference with the girls when they planned another round of baking. Mother explained that if they wanted to be in business, they should buy their own flour, sugar, and other ingredients. And they should include the cost of materials in pricing their cookies. Mother added they were welcome to continue using her oven. The prospect of a badly depleted "profit" may have dampened the ambition of our budding entrepreneurs, for they did not do any baking after that.

While I was a freshman in college I, too, had my eye on a business venture where the margin of profit appeared very promising. I thought my kid sister was such a neophyte in the cookie business, and I certainly felt I would do a great deal better. After all I had been a bootblack when I was in grade school. And I had even diversified my enterprises for I also got into selling old newspapers to the peanut vendor, scraps of shoe leather to the other boys for making slingshots, and trading my grandfather's discarded small quinine bottles for all kinds of things like marbles, bottle caps, and even a live hermit crab.

My new plan was to buy a piglet and give it to one of the farm tenant families to raise. I knew that since our pigs foraged by themselves part of the time, and their diet was supplemented with leftover food plus a little bit of rice bran, the cost of feeding was minimal. Thus, if the pig was sold after it was bigger, I

Entrusting my piglet to free enterprise.

could split the sale price with the farm family. I thought that was fair enough. I buy the piglet; they feed the pig and *presto*! I had a vision of blanketing the province with piglets entrusted to various tenant farmers. Think of the additional income to the farmers, and the profit that would come to me!

I saved some money, bought a piglet, and found a young couple at the farm who eagerly joined me for that venture. I counted the months and visualized my piglet hogging all the scraps at the farm and the tidbits in the forest. I touched base with the couple once in a while. They assured me that my investment was growing for it was eating like a pig! Their confidence was so encouraging that I began planning my next step, which was to recruit more families.

After about a year, I wondered if it was time to market our pig. I contacted my business partners. They told me that the pig had "died suddenly!" That was it, no explanation. My investment and my dreams crashed, just like that.

I should have known better. Landlords and tenant farmers have long played a game of cat and mouse with the harvest. The grind of poverty has taught some of our tenant farmers to be resourceful in order to survive. When the government or the landlords are not responsive to the needs of the poor, it is difficult to blame the oppressed who then learn to cut corners. I guess my piglet and I were caught in the process.

"The pig died suddenly!"

Enforcer

While I was growing up in Laoag, there was an assortment of local functionaries who were sup- posed to keep errant individuals in check. In a way they represented a non-formal network of reminders to insure that the norms of "proper" behavior were followed at school, at social events, in movie theaters, and, of course, at home. Some performed their assigned duties even-handedly; others had, I thought, an inflated view of their importance. The fol- lowing are samples of the "authority figures" that the children in Laoag had to contend with.

I remember stories told by Mother or Father about their respective eldest siblings who were expected to insure that the younger brothers and sisters behaved according to the family code of conduct. Most issues of concern were small things like who the siblings could associate with, what time of the day they should be home, how the girls should dress, or whether they could use a lipstick.

I was the firstborn within my immediate family, and also the first grandchild of the extended family on both Mother's and Father's side. This was a lot of responsibility. The downside, as I saw it, was that I was expected to be an example of good behavior to the younger siblings and cousins. Given my reputation for instigating mischief, I found this role-model business difficult to fulfill. I was usually the first suspect whenever some mischief occurred among the children within my extended family.

In the immediate neighborhood, how can I forget *Lakay* Ponsit, that impish little man, that self-appointed "animal doctor," and *aficionado* of fighting roosters, who also took it upon himself to be the elderly "pacifier" for the quarrelsome women in the neighborhood. When the women were engaged in verbal combat, usually in the afternoon when there was considerable consumption of *basi,* out he would come brandishing his *bolo* (machete), strutting around, and shouting at nobody in particular, only calling attention to himself. Since *Lakay* Ponsit, who was shorter than some of the women, looked a bit comical and had never hurt anybody, the women just ignored him. He was regarded as a pest by the women, a source of entertainment to the children, and never a threat to anybody.

I learned as a young boy in Laoag that there were people who were designated by law to maintain order within the whole community. The local police force was the respected agency of law enforcement that had that responsibility. In the 1930s, a policeman of Laoag had a khaki coat, matching trousers, and a hat styled very much like the Bobbies of London. He was armed with a revolver and a club. He was a figure to reckon with. The kids behaved when he was around, as did the quarrelsome women and the drunks of the neighborhood. Looking back, I wonder how a policeman could have stood the tropical heat in that uniform.

In school, our *Mama* Ti, the eldest sister of Father and also the principal of the elementary schools I attended, was definitely the disciplinarian of our extended family. Since the teachers were reluctant to punish me because I was the nephew of the principal, I was marched to her office, when the occasion warranted it, to have my open palms beaten with a wooden ruler by *Mama* Ti herself. I remember in general that I accepted the punishment, and even thought I deserved it. Luckily, none of the beatings ever seriously injured my fingers.

I was fortunate, too, that I was never subjected to the ordeal inflicted by that male teacher in the upper elementary grades where a misbehaving boy was asked to lower his trousers (in an all-boys class) for some beating on the posterior with a stick. Another teacher, who was a spinster, had her own style of punishment for the boys in the elementary grades. She would reach down slowly and pinch the inside part of the thigh right next to the private part of the misbehaving boy. Looking back, perhaps the boys in class were a bit unfair to that female teacher for suspecting that, because she was an old maid, her manner of punishing the boys was probably a source of vicarious gratification for her. Oh well, how our imaginations as kids ran wild sometimes.

In grade school even some students acted as authority figures when they were selected to serve as proctors during examination time. They were supposed to insure that no cheating occurred. We avoided making eye contact with them while we were taking the test for it aroused suspicion on the part of the proctor. So I made it a point to look at the ceiling, the board, or through the window, but never to make any eye contact with a proctor. They were petty functionaries indeed, but they made our lot as students that much more complicated.

Outside the school were other experiences with various forms of law enforcement. My brief role as an enforcer occurred when, as cub scouts, we were supposed to patrol the inner wall of the enclosure of the auditorium to insure that there were no people peeping through the *sawali* (woven bamboo) walls when there was a program inside and people were supposed to pay to get in. I still shudder when I recall poking a stick through the holes. I have sometimes asked myself, what if I had injured somebody's eye? What a senseless thing I did, misguided in my interpretation of my responsibility.

Later, when I was in the high school, I worked as a security guard at a warehouse. There were two of us, and we were armed with an automatic carbine. One evening my companion could not come to work, so I was by myself. I set up an army cot in front of the warehouse under an awning. Since it was *sel-lag* (full moon), visibility was relatively clear around the building. After midnight, when it was quiet except for an occasional *calesa* (horse-drawn carriage) passing by, I noticed someone scaling the five-foot-high concrete fence. The person climbed over the fence at a location about fifty feet from where I was. Because my cot was under the awning of the warehouse and shaded from the light of the moon, I speculated that the person may not have noticed me.

I thought I should make my presence known by moving forward into the light of the moon. I preferred for him to run away, and that would have been the end of it as far as I was concerned. But he continued walking slowly toward me. "Halt," I shouted. But what I intended as a booming voice of authority came out a bit squeaky, caused by a sudden dryness in my mouth and tightness in my throat. I was also ambivalent about the use of the gun, and a number of questions rushed through my mind. How much closer should I allow him before I did anything? Should I fire at him or just a warning shot toward the sky? If he ignored my warning shot, should I fire to disable him?

He was about twenty-five feet from me when I finally recognized the person. He was a mentally retarded boy who wandered about town during the day. Now he was probably looking for a place to sleep for the night. Realizing that he was harmless, I put the safe on the gun, and pointed it downward. When he finally stopped, I approached him and scolded him for putting himself at risk. I doubted, however, if that made any sense to him. He turned around without saying anything, climbed over the fence again, and was gone.

Other enforcers I have observed were more impulsive in the exercise of their authority and, in some cases, with harmful consequences. I remember a person who was assigned at a movie house to keep discipline within the theater. Some members of the audience occasionally got carried away. They would shout encouragement to the hero, voice their disdain for the villain, or warn an actor who was about to be ambushed. When the boisterous ones got out of hand, and started quarrelling, there was Berto in his khaki uniform and his hair slicked down like Rudolf Valentino's. His symbol of authority was his club, which he used readily when he pulled offending customers out of the movie theater.

But Berto's use of his club is mild compared to what another security guard did at the other cinema in town. It is difficult for me to forget what happened only a few days after the inauguration of a new movie house in Laoag called "Life Theater." It was a four-story building made of concrete, more impressive than the old "Cine Reyes" where Berto worked which was like a warehouse made of galvanized iron. Thus, a great deal of advertising and fanfare preceded the opening of the Life Theater.

I went to the new movie theater a few days after its inauguration. It was impressive indeed. One could still detect the smell of new concrete. The ticket seller and other attendants were in uniform, and so was the security guard. I handed my ticket to the attendant and was ushered into the *Entrada General* on the first floor. The chairs were new, no bedbugs yet, I thought, unlike Cine Reyes which had acquired the name of "Cine *Kiteb*" (Cine Bedbug). Even more important, the distinct odor from the toilets did not waft through the entire building as it did at the Cine Reyes. I settled down to watch the newsreel. It reminded me of the more expensive theaters in Manila that I remembered from my visits to the big city when I was still an elementary school pupil.

About thirty minutes into the movie, a loud bang came from the vicinity of the lobby. I got out of my seat, which was close to the entrance, to see what had caused the explosion. Right on the floor next to the stand of the ticket attendant was a man sprawled with his face down. Meanwhile, two men were restraining the security guard. As recounted by one of the bystanders, the guard had just fatally shot a man who was allegedly advancing toward the guard with a knife. A knife was indeed on the floor not too far from the body of the slain person. What an inauguration for a building called, ironically, "Life Theater!"

Little did I know, however, that my experience with "big time" enforcement of international proportions would come decades later when I was assigned in Swaziland in 1979 under a United States Agency for International Development (USAID) and Eastern Michigan University (EMU) contract. Tired from the long flight from Ann Arbor through London and Johannesburg, and finally to Manzini, Swaziland, I was glad to arrive at the assigned dwelling which was going to be "home" for the next two years. I had my own three-bedroom bungalow, one of six other units built specially for members of the EMU project. After unpacking my suitcase, I showered and settled for the night. Sleep did not come easily, partly because of the jet lag and from the excitement of being in Swaziland. I finally dozed off.

Sometime in the night I was awakened by a series of loud explosions that shook my bed and rattled the windows. I did not turn on the light. I just lay quietly in the dark wondering what had happened. It was dead quiet outside after that except for some dogs barking. At dawn a few tense hours later, I ventured outside to find out about the explosion. With a glimmer of early morning light, I could see there were people gathered on the street in front of the bungalows. Some of the women were still in their nightgowns. The people were obviously agitated and spoke in whispers.

I approached one of the men and inquired about what had happened. He heard, he told me, that a couple of houses not too far away had been blown up. Was there an accident? I pursued. He looked agitated, and was clearly reluctant to say more. He did not know, he said.

I learned later that members of the South African Armed Forces had come to Swaziland, and had bombed and demolished a couple of houses which were presumed to be occupied at the time. A few days before, an electric power station in South Africa had been blown up and some members of the African National Congress (ANC), then campaigning for an end to apartheid in South Africa, were assumed to be responsible. Whether there were any casualties in that South African incident, I do not remember. The houses in Swaziland were said to have been the hiding place of some members of the ANC. If what I heard and read in the papers were true, it was equally amazing to me that I never heard of any formal protest by the government of Swaziland against what was essentially a violation of its national boundaries by another country. It was difficult to avoid the impression that an all-powerful South African Armed Force in that part of the world could, with apparent impunity, enforce its will. In a sense, the long shadow of apartheid extended to Swaziland, and there I was a witness to an episode in the struggle of an oppressed people for freedom. I was at the very beginning of a two-year assignment in Swaziland. What else, I thought, was in store for me?

Roadblock

As creatures of habit we do not like roadblocks. Especially if we are the drivers of vehicles, be it cars, trucks or even animal-drawn carts. But we also understand that roadblocks are there for a purpose, maybe for a road repair, investigation of a crime or an accident, or for security. Grudgingly, we take a different route after uttering the almost ritualistic complaint about roadblocks and one-way streets. Pedestrians, on the other hand, have more flexibility circumventing barriers, at their own risk, of course.

When the Japanese Army occupied Laoag, they set up roadblocks in various locations to control the civilians' access to and exit from the town. The places that were open were guarded by soldiers and impressively fortified with machine guns, their barrels sticking through openings between the sandbags. A sentry armed with a rifle and fixed bayonet was always on guard. He checked pedestrians who came through. If people were riding in a cart, they were expected to get out of the vehicle, line up, and bow to the sentry in unison. The sentry bowed, too, to reciprocate the gesture. Suspicious circumstances were checked more closely, otherwise people were signaled to proceed on their way. Not much time lost usually, but certainly the whole procedure was an affront to people's dignity, especially to those who strongly resented the Japanese occupation.

There is one roadblock incident that I remember with particular clarity. That was when I decided to go to the barrio of *Camangaan* (which means "where there are mangoes") about two miles east of Laoag, to retrieve my bicycle which had been appropriated, without my permission, by Moreng, a cousin who was in a guerrilla unit somewhere in that vicinity.

I was determined to get my bicycle back because it was my first adult-sized bicycle. I had built it myself, and I was proud of it. Weeks ago, I had bought parts such as pedals, tires, saddle, etc., from different people and assembled the whole thing on an old frame I salvaged from the dump. After I had sanded and painted it with some leftover paint I found in the house, it looked quite nice. It was in running condition by the time I put it away in the storeroom to allow the paint to dry properly. Meanwhile, I went to the farm in Surrate, Dingras, east of Laoag, for a few days to visit my family who were still there on evacuation.

Needless to say, I had been eager to get back to Laoag to try my "new" bike. After exchanging the usual greetings at the house after my return, I headed straight to the storeroom to see my bicycle. It was not in its place where I left it. I inquired if someone moved it to another location. The houseboy, *Lakay*

Itong, told me Moreng had taken my bicycle. "For a ride?" I inquired. I was hoping it was just a temporary inconvenience. "No," he said. "He is gone. I do not know where, but I think he is on his way to join a guerilla unit somewhere in the east." I was very angry and felt violated. I also felt frustrated since I could not think of how I could ever recover it.

Days turned to weeks, and no sign of my bicycle. Later on, I heard that some of our relatives on my paternal grandmother's side were in *Camangaan* for evacuation. I entertained the slim hope that Moreng had had the decency to leave the bicycle with them on his way farther east. Without telling anybody, I planned a visit to those relatives on my own. I figured that if I started on foot immediately after breakfast, and if I cut through farms and back roads to avoid Japanese patrols, I could probably reach my destination by noon. That meant I could be back in Laoag in time for dinner without anyone in the house knowing where I had been.

One additional consideration for the trip was how I could bypass the Japanese checkpoint at the Rizal Street/Vintar Road junction. I wanted to avoid the indignity of bowing to the Japanese sentry. Other roads in that direction were blocked because the Japanese intended to channel all the traffic going east through that particular checkpoint. I decided to cross a roadblock that I thought was effectively hidden from the sentry by a high rise in the road that separated the two points. The day before my trip, I walked to the unguarded roadblock where I planned to cross to see how it was constructed, and also to estimate how much time and effort it would take to scale it.

On the day of the trip, I left the house immediately after breakfast and reached the roadblock in fifteen minutes. As I was preparing to scale the structure, I was surprised to see about a dozen other young men who were also scaling it. From their athletic build, serious demeanor, and the efficient way in which they climbed the obstacle, I assumed they were guerillas. It gave me a sense of security to think that I probably would not be alone in my hike eastward.

Once on the other side of the barrier and crossing the road flanked by the other young men, I realized one serious shortcoming in my choice of a roadblock to climb. While the sentry could not see me, neither could I see what might come from that direction. Suddenly, to my horror, a truck appeared over the rise on the road. It was a Japanese Army vehicle complete with a machine gun mounted on top of the cab and a number of soldiers behind that machine gunner! The truck was probably at least five hundred yards away, and it accelerated down the slope as soon as they spotted what surely appeared to be a highly suspicious group. We scattered like ants.

I ran as fast as I could and went through a fence gate before the truck could turn into the side road. It is likely that the Japanese soldiers could not have seen where we all went. I climbed the stairs of a house constructed of *nipa* palm and bamboo, bigger than those in the farms. It was quiet and I could smell a delicate fragrance. I surprised a young woman who was taking a bath in the *bansag* (an open section sometimes between house and kitchen for washing and drying dishes). She had a *dwa na-ig* (sarong) on. She was, as would be expected, horrified, and was about to scream but I gestured with my forefinger to my lips.

I surprised a bathing beauty. 1943.

A man came hurriedly out of a room. I explained quickly that the Japanese were looking for a group that had just scaled the roadblock. We could hear a truck passing by, and then stopping probably about four houses down. We could also hear the Japanese soldiers. My surprised hosts understood, and did not question me further.

I asked the man to bring out a pair of scissors, and instructed him to start cutting my hair. This was, I thought, the best and quickest way to make it appear that I was a member of the family should the Japanese come into their house. I sat on a chair. The man held the comb and a pair of scissors, ready to cut my hair if any of the soldiers came up. Meanwhile, the young lady scampered into one of the rooms to get dressed. It seemed like an eternity before the truck finally drove away.

I waited for another half hour. I thanked the people at the house, looked around before I went into the street, and resumed my journey. I walked as casually as I could and continued through the fields long enough to avoid the Japanese in case they decided to wait elsewhere.

I stopped in a few houses to ask where I could find the Tumanengs, my paternal grandmother's family name. Eventually, I was directed to a cluster of houses farther down the road. My relatives were indeed surprised to see me. But to my disappointment, they did not know Moreng's whereabouts, and did not know anything about a bicycle. It was noon by then, and they insisted I have lunch before I returned to Laoag. It was very nice to be with them, all the more so because of what I had just gone through, although I did not mention it. Meeting relatives and feeling safe in their midst was comforting.

After lunch I thanked them and returned to Laoag. I followed the main road, and did what I was supposed to do when I reached the checkpoint. I bowed to the sentry, crossing my fingers as I did so and hoping that he would not recognize me from the morning's episode. He waved me on.

The price of defeat.

Primitive Justice

When I read or hear about allegations of continuing corruption in the government of the Philippines, I sometimes wonder what it would take to inject discipline and more concern for social justice in our society. We claim to be a democratic nation because we hold local and national elections periodically. This ritual, however, has never impressed me. It seems to be nothing more than a charade riddled with allegations of dishonesty, bribery, corruption, and violence.

It is not very encouraging that we seemed to exhibit more discipline (or was it fear?) when we were subjected to the uncompromising, authoritarian iron fist of the Japanese forces when they occupied the Philippines. If that is what it takes for Filipinos to abide by the law, what a sad commentary it is on our ability, or inability, to govern ourselves. I remember how the looting of Chinese stores in Laoag was controlled only after two men were shot on the spot by Japanese soldiers. Fear seemed to be a factor also in forcing the people to comply with regulations to dispose of their garbage properly, to clean up after the animals that littered the streets (especially the horses that pulled the *calesas*), and for the young people to get up early in the morning to perform exercises prescribed by the Japanese.

There is another event that has stuck in my mind through all the decades that have passed since the Japanese occupation. It was a savage exhibition of the absolute power of the conqueror over the vanquished.

After the Japanese occupation forces in Laoag finally established some degree of stability, they created a puppet civilian government including a local police force. We were told that irregularities and corruption on the part of the Filipino officials, including the police, were not to be tolerated by the Japanese authorities. Given the treatment levied upon the people who did not abide by the policies of the Japanese, such as the previously mentioned shooting of looters on the spot, the slapping or the extended forced exposure to the sun for those who failed to bow to a Japanese sentry, there was no reason to believe otherwise.

A particular Filipino policeman was reported to have been abusing his authority by intimidating people in the *barrios* and extracting bribes whenever he could. Matters got to the point where these alleged abuses were ultimately reported to the Japanese authorities. News about the arrest and imprisonment of the policeman spread quickly through the town. It was not long, however, before the town was alerted through the *bando* (a town crier with a drummer who went from one block to another to announce news of importance to the neighborhood) that the prisoner had escaped. The escape route of the fugitive was limited. To venture far from the town, he would have had to contend with the guerillas who would have been only too glad to get hold of a "Japanese collaborator." I believe it was only two or three days after the escape when the *bando* announced that the Japanese had recaptured the fugitive, and that there would be a public execution by the riverside at the foot of the Laoag Gilbert Bridge.

I was only fourteen years old then, and I debated whether I had the stomach to watch a public execution. But when I saw people, including younger ones like me, beginning to converge towards the designated site, I followed the crowd almost as if I couldn't do otherwise. It was a cloudy afternoon, and people (probably no more than a hundred) were assembled in a large circle around an empty spot by the riverbank. It was a very quiet crowd, and we did not wait very long before a squad of fully armed Japanese soldiers arrived in a truck with the prisoner. His hands were tied behind his back. They proceeded to the partially open area encircled by the crowd. The prisoner was told to kneel. I did not know whether I wanted to look or turn the other way at that point. The prisoner who was kneeling was kicked in the stomach and, as he bent over, the Japanese soldier brought down his saber with a powerful and swift stroke over the prisoner's neck. The prisoner fell forward and quivered briefly. The Japanese left the body where it fell, and exited immediately in their truck. There were screams from the crowd as soon as the Japanese left the area. I assumed those who screamed were relatives, for a small group rushed forward with a blanket that they draped over the fallen body. I could not see much after that because the crowd closed in.

The covered body was placed on a bamboo platform that was later carried on the shoulders of four men. They struggled briefly as they negotiated the sandy riverbank. They continued to carry him that way on the street towards the western side of the town where, I assumed, the man had resided. I followed the crowd. Someone occasionally shouted to the onlookers along the street to tell them who it was. When we reached the house, there was more screaming. I reached only as far as the top of the bamboo stairway. I tried to look in but it was too crowded. I left at that point.

I struggled with a lot of strong emotions as I walked home. I remember that I was scared. But it was not only from having witnessed the brutality of a public execution. The screaming also haunted me. I could still hear it even as I walked away from the house. I assumed the policeman had been a husband and that he had children. Life is so precious, I thought, and yet it can so easily be taken away. I never told my family where I had been that afternoon.

Even as a young boy, I felt surely that the public execution I had witnessed was a savage and a primitive form of punishment. Over the years, the event has resonated with me in terms of the choices we have as a people in the way we govern ourselves—whether that be through fear of those who control the forces of violence, or by internal discipline manifested by honest elections, less corruption in public life, and more compassion for the oppressed. I believe we have the ability to govern ourselves with a greater sense of fairness and justice for all. Whether that day will ever come will ultimately depend upon the people themselves.

The Professional Mourners

After she covered her face with a scarf and draped her arms over the open casket, the old woman uttered a gut-wrenching wail that scared the daylights out of me, then an eight-year-old boy. I looked around quickly to see the expression of the adults seated around the *sala* hoping to find some sympathy for my predicament. For the most part they appeared oblivious to the drama unfolding in the center of the room—the open coffin with a body in it, and the wailing woman. They seemed absorbed in their own conversations. That made me feel even more isolated, so I moved closer to three elderly women huddled together in one corner of the room because they seemed to be the only ones who looked focused on what was going on.

From what I could make out, their conversation was partly an assessment of the woman who was wailing. *"Talaga nga ma-yat ti panagdung-aw na,"* they muttered. ("She really mourns well.") The wailer continued for another five minutes, and the segments I could understand included praises for the good qualities of the deceased, how he was going to be missed, and so on. Then she stopped suddenly, stood up, and came over to where the three other women were seated. She calmly suggested, *"Sica metten, Kasinsin."* ("It is your turn, Cousin.") Wide-eyed, I stared at the face of the wailer. I was puzzled that there seemed to be no trace of crying. She reached for a mixture of *betel* nut (areca nut) and *betel* pepper leaf. She popped a wad into her mouth, and she asked if the other women had eaten. Food, incidentally, is one of the attractions of events like this. It was *Lola* Sabina who told me later that the women in the corner were professional mourners who were hired to do their thing. She added that it would be a source of embarrassment for the family of a deceased if nobody did any crying. These professional mourners took care of that!

I did my own crying when my *Lolo* Justo passed away. It happened when the professional photographer insisted that the three grandsons (Erning then eight years old, Romeo six, and I eight) sit close to *Lolo* Justo's body. I can tell you that *Lolo* had been a good friend of mine when he was alive, but sitting right next to his corpse was a different story altogether. Truth to be told, I cried out of fear, but the old folks were very touched because they thought I was grief-stricken. Meanwhile I wondered if the picture-taking would ever end.

Despite my discomfort at Lolo Justo's wake, in grade school I enjoyed watching picture-taking at funerals. Perhaps it was morbid curiosity. The Laoag Central School which I attended from grades one through five was right across from the Philippine Independent Church on Rizal Street, also known as the Aglipayan Church. I recall there were funeral services held there almost every day, sometimes twice a day. And when these events coincided with our school recess or when classes were over for the day, it was always tempting to cross the street with my classmates and gawk at the family picture-taking in front of the church.

The open casket would be propped up at a forty-five-degree angle for a better view with the lens and, I suppose, to enhance the effect of a "family portrait." We always wanted to get as close as possible to look at the face, provided it did not smell. In that tropical heat, if the embalming had not been done properly, there were times when we did not cross the street because the smell reached us even as far as the school grounds.

The scarier the faces were, with their sunken eyes and exposed teeth, the more fascinated we were, even if the image stayed with us for days and made us avoid being alone in the dark. For us curious kids maybe it was the closest thing we had to something like a horror movie. And that may have had some long-lasting and reverse effect on me for I now avoid, whenever I can, going to funeral parlors for viewing. However, because of social conventions, that is not always possible.

When I was still new in the US, my cousin invited me to attend a viewing in one of the funeral parlors in Chicago. My first reaction was to decline, but I decided it was probably a good opportunity for some "participant-observation," one of the fancy terms I had just picked up from one of my classes on research methods. So there we went. The setup at the funeral parlor was very different from what I remembered way back in Laoag. There were, for example, no official wailers, feasting, or betel nuts, and the benches were arranged as in a chapel. Since there were a number of people, there was a line that moved slowly past the open casket. My cousin suggested we join the line after she signed something on a table near the door. I told myself that would be all right for I would just look straight ahead as I passed by the casket. I certainly did not want to be reminded of those gruesome faces in a coffin in front of the church from my elementary school days. Unfortunately, when I was standing next to the casket, the line stopped! It was a traffic jam, and there I was caught in the middle of it. Firmly I kept looking straight ahead not even a glance at the dead face which was barely three feet from me. It seemed like time stood still, but that curiosity that I had as a boy began to take over. I turned my head ever so slowly, and I looked at the face. To my relief, it was unlike those scary images I remembered. The face was actually that of a beautiful young woman who looked as if she was asleep, and I relaxed. Nonetheless, to this day I still prefer to remember people as they were, with all their frailties, but very much alive, active, and well.

Speedy Gonzales

Since some Filipino houses were not well protected against the intrusion of mice and rats, we had to find ways of coping and co-existing. Cats helped a bit. But not after they became old and lazy, and discovered that siesta did not exclusively have to be after lunch. Besides hoping that house cats would earn their keep, we also learned to be respectful. That is, we learned not to harass the mice and the rats, for they have very long memories and can be very vindictive! At least that is what the old folks told us eager young hunters with our slingshots.

I remember as a preschool boy chasing after the occasional mouse or rat that would scamper on the floor along the wall from one part of the house to another. *Baket* Mat-ti, the housemaid, reminded me that it was not good to offend the mice for they can harm us in return. My elders who were in the *sala* did nothing to correct *Baket* Mat-ti so I interpreted their silence as endorsement of what she said. After about week, it was found that some of the pillows piled high for storage during the day were full of holes, apparently the work of mice. *Baket* Mat-ti was quick with her verdict that the holes were unmistakable manifestations of rodent retribution, and she reminded me once again that I should never harass the mice or rats.

Years later when I was in grade school, I remember the provisional kitchen and dining attachment to the Segundo house that was built for Mom and Dad's growing family. The ceiling of the dining area was made of nicely woven bamboo with a herringbone design. The rectangular dining table was big enough for six with Father seated at the head and Mother at the opposite end. When we ate, one of the maids stood by the table with a *bogao*, a short bamboo pole with a cluster of colored paper ribbons at one end that was swayed over the table to keep the flies away. Father made sure, too, that the dining area was kept clean, food stored properly as much as possible, and no quarters were given to mice or rats. At least that was what he wanted. Mother jokingly reminded him, just as *Baket* Mat-ti reprimanded me years back, not to antagonize the mice or rats. Father dismissed those words of caution as a lot of nonsense. I found his logic reassuring because I had never really accepted that my mice-chasing was the reason they had eaten holes in the pillows years ago.

One dinnertime, with Father presiding at his usual place at the table, there was an interruption in the form of droplets pattering swiftly down on the head of Father. The liquid seemed to come down in greater amount even as he moved out of the way quickly, looked up to the ceiling, and loudly cursed at the source. It was obviously a rat that was relieving itself and, of all

"Rats and mice have a long memory, and they can be vindictive."

places, right on Father's head and dinner plate. All of us looked at Father in shock. We had never heard such outpouring of expletives from him. My mother realized what had happened. She covered her mouth to contain herself, but was convulsed with laughter nonetheless. Father continued to swear in the direction of the ceiling. The dining table was cleared and cleaned immediately while Father went to the bathroom to take a shower!

For a few days after that, I noticed Father always looked up briefly when he sat down. He would mumble something as if he was saying grace, or was it something less reverent? Pointedly he did not look at Mother while he tried to maintain his dignity as *pater familia*. Meanwhile, Mother would glance toward him and then look at us. I could see that she felt like laughing again, but she knew better.

Decades later in our house in Quezon City, Father, who was then retired, told me about a mouse that had been tormenting him. "What insolence," he said. "Sometimes when I am reading the paper, I see him run across the floor showing no fear whatsoever!" I asked him what he had done. He said he always gave chase and he had taken to keeping a fly swatter next to him in readiness. Father had finally named this impudent adversary "Speedy Gonzales." Weeks passed and the saga between Father and Speedy continued. Father recalled he finally cornered Speedy with no place to escape. "I raised the fly swatter and was about to put an end to that pesky creature that had been tormenting me. I think Speedy knew it was the end. The tiny thing sat there and looked at me. I just did not have the heart to strike him. I let him go."

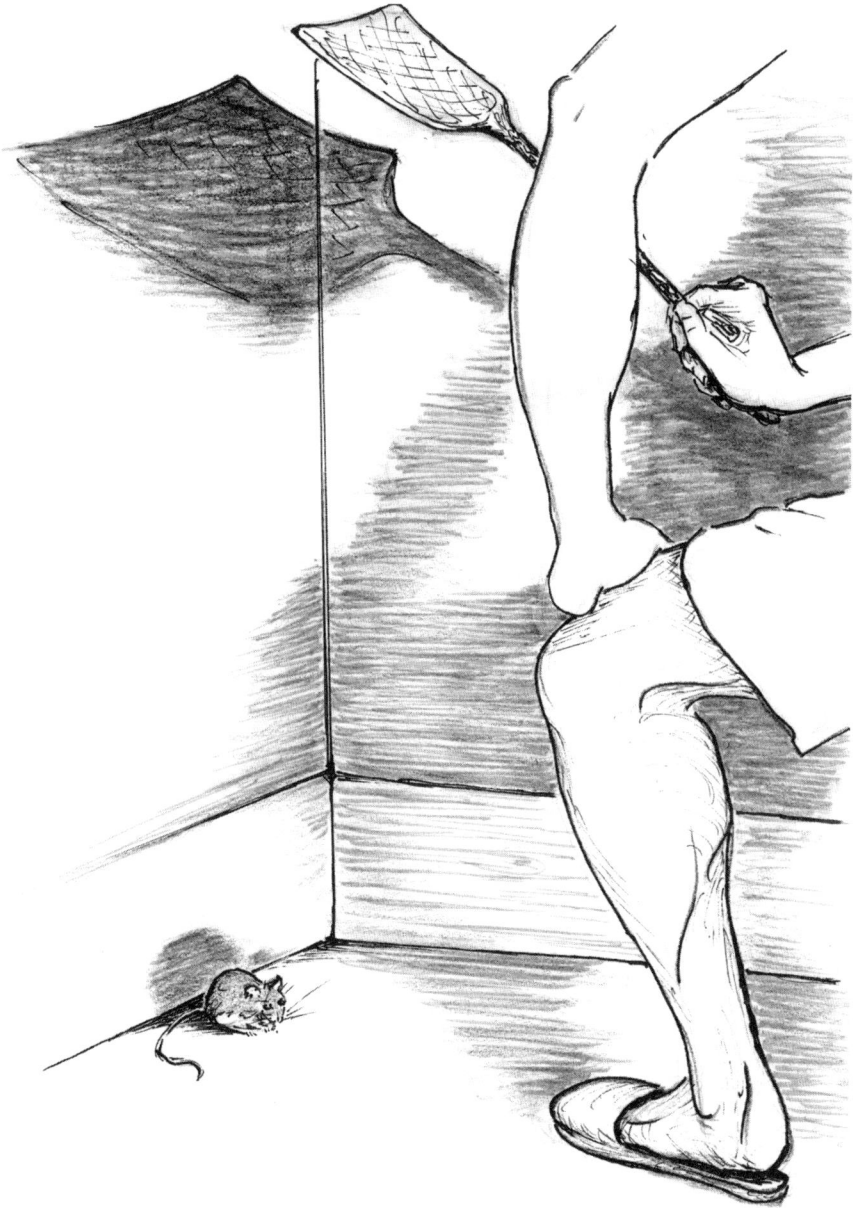

"I finally got him cornered!"

Shoes

R ight after the end of the Second World War when schools
had recently reopened, students and teachers alike
made do with the scarcity of many things, including
school supplies and clothing. Therefore, we were grateful for
relief organizations that extended surplus goods to the community from the US Air Force base outside the town. The men
and boys in particular benefited from surplus uniforms, and
one would have noticed a lot of ill-fitting khaki shirts, trousers,
and shoes among both the students and the teachers on the
school grounds and in the classrooms. A welcome variation
from this sea of khakis was the occasional white shirt that was
made out of discarded parachutes.

So there we were in a horticulture class under Mr. Asuncion
(nicknamed *Musa Sapientum* by the students), most of us in
our khakis sitting on improvised benches under the trellises to
shade us from the sun. With a blackboard leaned against one of
the posts, Mr. Asuncion gave his lecture on a variety of topics

such as seed selection, crop rotation, fertilizers, mulching, pruning, grafting, budding, cross-pollination, and so on.

Shorter than most of the students in his all-boys senior high school class, Mr. Asuncion must have felt limited sometimes in his ability to command authority and impose discipline. While we, his students, were aware of this possible predicament, most of us did not take advantage of it. At that time in the 1940s, it is fair to say that we still observed the traditional respect that was accorded to a teacher. And Mr. Asuncion was also regarded as knowledgeable in his field, and a gentleman in speech and manner. But there was always the occasional bully in class who liked to show off by carrying on, for instance, with his private conversation even while the teacher was giving his lecture.

Mr. Asuncion had his limit, too, and he would politely ask in a non-confrontational way, "Let's be quiet now, everybody." But the bully kept on talking, and we paid attention more closely when Mr. Asuncion finally stopped his presentation and stared at the offending student who was much taller than the teacher. Did it finally come to a showdown? We waited in suspense, a welcome change from the lecture about fertilizers.

Mr. Asuncion finally displayed real anger. In cases like this, sometimes we wondered if the small man had some hidden skills in the martial arts that he might have learned in college. But being the gentleman that he was, he vented his anger instead against one of the center bamboo posts of the trellis; he delivered with authority what appeared to be a powerful kick as in Thai boxing. Fortunately for the post, he missed it, nearly losing his balance, and his oversized and heavy GI shoe went sailing over the heads of the students. After regaining his balance and dignity, he finally joined in the hearty laughter of the class.

It is still a source of amusement for me to remember other observations about shoes as I was growing in Laoag. For instance, some people thought they could tell one's economic background if one did not own a pair of shoes, for surely we did not have folks then who went barefoot just to make a political statement. On the other end of the social scale were those who preferred imported goods, "colonial mentality" as some academics called it. "American-made" was for those who could afford them. And not just American-made, mind you, for it had to be Florsheim, Allen Edmonds, or something like that. They might even take off their shoes to expose the brand name to convince doubting Thomases.

Squeaky shoes did not seem to bother those who regarded the noise as a fitting proclamation that they were the proud owners of a new pair of shoes. But wearing them with their "Sunday best" when they walked down the aisle to attend mass evoked reproving glares from other people who were probably distracted from their prayers. Equally distracting were shoes that had been newly re-soled with locally tanned leather and were noted for a smell that could not even be masked by burning incense.

But my mother had concerns other than squeaky shoes or smelly leather soles. She knew that my feet were growing, hence, a newly purchased pair for me was usually two sizes too big, for I "would soon grow into them." She padded each shoe generously with cotton, and I kept stubbing my new shoes for it took time to get used to the extra inch beyond my feet. Given concerns such as these about shoes, it is just as well that most of our farmers in Ilocos Norte preferred to go barefoot.

But the choice to go without shoes was not always possible. When a law was passed before 1941 to conscript soldiers for a newly formed Philippine Army, our able-bodied young men from the farms soon found themselves marching awkwardly as drill sergeants shouted *kanigid, kanawan, kanigid, kanawan* (left, right, left, right). So additional attraction for the townfolk when there was a military parade was to watch some of the poor soldiers struggle with their new pair of shoes—some limping, others stubbing their toes against irregularities on the road. But the new recruits solved that promptly when they went home on weekends. With a pole on their shoulders, they carried a small bag and a pair of army shoes dangling at the end as they proudly walked home in their bare feet!

Mom and Dad in the garden of the old Samonte house, late 1920s.

At the house in Ann Arbor, 1960s.

Cousin Erning and the author at the garden of the
old Samonte house, early 1930s.

A visit to Daraga, Albay, Philippines. Front L to R: nieces Shelah, Sarah, Sehrish and their mother, Cousin May. Back L to R: Auntie Alice, Judy, the author, Tio Gil (brother of Mother, husband of Auntie Alice, and father of cousin May), and Roly, my brother. 2005.

Siblings of the author with their respective spouses. Front L to R: Lito Gorospe and Astrid (Samonte), Judy and the author, Francia Samonte Scales. Back L to R: Roly Samonte and Lilian (Sakamoto), Amy (Samonte) and Antonio Benavides. 2005.

Playing with a neighborhood kitten.

Cristina entertaining her
little sister, Cindy.

Judy and Cristina at the Arboretum, Ann Arbor, Michigan.

Visit to Solsona, Ilocos Notre.

Cristina and Cynthia with their cousins during a trip to the Philippines. From L to R: Cristina, Alana, May, Caroline, Cindy, Marites, and Winnie.

**Mom and Dad with grandchildren at their house
in Quezon City, Philippines.**

Part II
Getting to Know You

Celebrating
San Guillermo

T he celebration of the town fiesta was a big event in
Filipino towns. Sometimes it lasted for a week beyond
the day of the patron saint for whom the fiesta was
observed. Special services were held in the church, and there
were religious processions. Public schools participated in a
variety of activities such as parades and folk dances. Different
professions and business organizations sponsored special programs for the evening dances at the auditorium. Booths were
set up in the tennis court to exhibit products from different
towns of the province. I must not forget the different rides and
games like a Ferris wheel, carousel, tent shows that featured
"freaks" of all kinds like a "spider child" complete with a web
made out of rope, the ever-present "fattest lady," and many
gambling tables.

In Laoag the town fiesta was truly the biggest event of the
year. The locals opened their homes to visitors, some of whom
might drop by for short visits, while others stayed for several

days if they were from out of town. Especially exciting for us boys who were in the upper grades of elementary school were nice-looking girls who came among our visitors.

A friend related an incident that had occurred at their house while a family with a beautiful daughter was visiting. On the third night, when everybody had bedded down after another busy day, the stillness of the evening was shattered by a scream from the direction of the visiting girl's room. Lights were turned on, and people were up in the living room bewildered and alarmed about the commotion. Soon it was revealed that someone had tried to sneak into the bedroom of the visiting daughter. The hosts were, needless to say, highly embarrassed.

With all the excitement going on, it was also noted, according to my friend, that one person was conspicuously missing. That person was my friend's older brother. It was discovered that he was apparently fast asleep in another room. He was fully covered with a blanket, even though it was a warm night, and appeared to be oblivious to what was going on. His mother picked up the broom. She delivered some telling blows to the "sleeping" brother, accompanied by a few well-chosen expletives. Do not underestimate mothers. I think they sometimes know more than they let on. My friend's brother had a rude "awakening" indeed. The brother got up quickly, did not offer any protest, but hightailed it out of the house in his underwear.

I would not be surprised if the brother, during his hasty and ignominious flight, thought it would have been far safer to spend a nickel to ogle the "fattest lady" at the carnival, and for another nickel he could have, for good measure, plotted a less risky future with a visit to the fortuneteller. At any rate, this was probably more excitement than that family anticipated for the town fiesta.

Do not underestimate mothers!

Olympics At High Noon

The debilitating summer heat slowed activities at noon in Laoag. Sensible folks took their *siesta*, laborers took time off for a little nap, work animals rested in the shade while they chewed their cud, and dogs slept. It was only the neighborhood boys who congregated under the shade of the *acacia* tree and wondered what to do.

Boredom and creativity.

The long summer vacation, while it was always welcomed initially by most school children, became quite a challenge after a month or so. Open-ended days without scheduled activities became monotonous. There were fruit trees to raid once in a while. An expedition to the nearby woods with our *tirador* or *palsi-it* (slingshot) was fun, and so were competitions with *bolintic* (marbles), *sunay* (wooden top), and with *il-law* (kites). Sometimes we flew with *medro* (powdered bulb glass pasted to the string) to cut competitors' lines. A trip to the river for a swim was also a favorite. Going to the movies was even better, but that was out of the question for most of the boys who could not afford five or ten centavos a day. Ordinarily the boys in the neighborhood did not have that kind of money, except for those lucky enough to be engaged in such activities as shining shoes, as I did when I was in grade school, being an errand boy, or delivering newspapers. Games that we enjoyed occasionally, like softball, *sipa* (played like volleyball but with a ball woven from a vine called *rattan*), "football" with an old tennis ball, were too strenuous even to contemplate when we were in the midday tropical sun.

Under the shade of the tree we would chit-chat and speculate. One time I remember somebody proposed a competition to determine who could pee the farthest! That galvanized everybody's interest. We laughed at the idea at first. Then the older boys became more serious about it. They set up a "ground rule." That is, they drew a line on the ground as a base from which "delivery" would be made. They also excluded those of us who were just seven and eight years old. I did not understand the rationale for that exclusion, unless there was some kind of an understanding about the caliber of the instrument that could be used in the contest, and the assumption that the older boys would have been at an advantage. Anyway it was the older kids, ten to fourteen years old, who were the eligible contestants. The five of us younger ones stood on the sidelines as eager spectators.

One by one the performers stepped to the line, the "ground rule." The others carefully checked that he did not step beyond it. The contestants observed carefully the delivery of each one, and tried to improve on it. The system that seemed to emerged included the following: (1) keep the tailwind behind you, (2) wait for a favorable breeze, (3) store the ammunition in the foreskin, which ballooned a little bit, and (4) quickly thrust the hip forward coordinated with a strong squeeze of the stored ammunition through a controlled little opening of the foreskin. It appeared it was the skill in coordinating all these that really produced the distance. But all these finer points of the rules of engagement were soon disregarded as the contestants turned combatants and started aiming at each other. That made it more exciting for us bystanders, who had to get out of the way quickly lest we got caught in a case of friendly fire. The combatants soon ran out of ammunition, and a truce followed.

Although I was neither a contestant nor a combatant that time, I recognized that here was another opportunity to gain status among the boys in the neighborhood. I knew it was only a matter of time, and I would soon be eligible for the contest. Thus, in the privacy of our garden behind the trees, I practiced secretly. I made a few adjustments here and there. Even after a few more trial runs, it was with some disappointment that I had to admit to myself I was not really Olympic material for such an event. I just could not make the qualifying distance.

Two For One

W hile I was assigned in various countries overseas under contract with the USAID, I would live in either a house or an apartment by myself. This was a situation that frequently caused a stir in the neighborhood, especially among some of the women. Even the driver from our North Yemen project was kind enough to suggest that I should have a live-in maid, and informed me that he knew of a young and "nice-looking" Ethiopian girl who was a good worker. In Swaziland where I was assigned from 1979 through 1981, I remember a few knocks at my door on weekends and in the evenings. It was a situation that I had to deal with delicately so as not to compromise myself and, just as important, not to antagonize anybody. Humor sometimes helped to resolve these awkward encounters.

Unfortunately, living alone also attracted other characters. My place of work in Manzini, Swaziland, was close to the housing compound. I walked to work if the weather was nice, and did the same at noon when I went home for lunch. When I got home one day, the back door was open and there were a few scattered items on the floor. It dawned on me then that the place had been burglarized. Checking around quickly revealed a lot of missing items: radio, tape recorder, and speakers from the living room. Taken from my bedroom were clothes, an extra pair of shoes, and photo equipment including a Leica camera and lenses, two Nikon camera bodies and lenses, and a half-frame Olympus camera and a number of lenses. Adding insult to injury, an expensive soft leather suitcase I had just bought in Japan was taken also, presumably to carry all that loot from my place! The usual police investigation at the premises followed. Nothing came of it, and the investigator suggested I should go to the police station to file a report.

At the police station, I was asked to submit a list of my missing items along with an estimate of their value. Before completing my report, the police investigator asked a few basic questions like name and address. That was expected enough, but I was not prepared when he asked what my "tribe" was. After reflecting on the question, I thought "American" was probably the most logical response. His next question was, "Who is your chief?" I said, "President Carter." He seemed satisfied with that, too, and my police report was completed.

Fortunately, that report came in handy when I called Judy in Michigan to check if our Ann Arbor home insurance covered my loss abroad. I did not expect anything really, but they told Judy that they would cover it if my legal residence was still Michigan and if I had a police report. I was actually quite surprised when the insurance company reimbursed the replacement value of what was stolen!

My big problem after that, however, was the sense of vulnerability that I experienced, especially at night. It felt like I was being watched, and I had a few restless and sleepless nights. In an effort to bolster my confidence, I drove to South Africa intending to buy a handgun. The salesman asked if I had a government permit to buy a firearm, which I did not. I drove back to my place without the weapon I wanted. But I wondered if obtaining a gun would do any good anyway since I would be reluctant to shoot anybody. I chose instead an arsenal of *knob-kerrie*s (wooden clubs used by the Swazis as a weapon) beside my bed to sustain my self-confidence.

Dealing with the persistent, enterprising, and amorous women was a more "tricky" matter. A knock at the door in the evening might be followed by a polite and civil conversation with the lady, but always at the door, without letting her in. One visitor reminded me that listening to the radio was not much company. It never went further than the conversation on my threshold, and I always expressed my appreciation for their "thoughtfulness."

There was a particularly determined one, however, who was my neighbor and who was also a sales girl in the grocery store where I bought my supplies. She had a lot of opportunity to see me. She was persistent, but she was also good-natured about it.

One time at the grocery store, she followed me around pretending to rearrange the merchandise. I decided to humor her a bit. I told her that one of my colleagues was staying with me for a while before he got his own house. I added that he had quite a reputation with women and suggested that it might be a good time for her to come and pay a visit so that there would be two men for her. She was wide-eyed as she listened intently. I embellished a little bit more. I added that I had seen when he opened his suitcase, a whip and a mallet, and that he just winked at me when I asked him if he was planning to go on a safari. I "confided" that since my colleague impressed me as a rough fellow, I was really concerned about her safety. She left me without saying anything. I continued my grocery shopping. Meanwhile, I was hoping that maybe I had finally discouraged her.

Before I was finished shopping, however, she appeared again. She said, "My girl friend will come with me!" I had to think of a good comeback for that one. The best I could do was to tell her that I would have to check with my colleague's schedule first. That seemed reasonable enough to her, and I was out of the grocery as quickly as possible. It was then close to the end of my assignment in that country, and I left Swaziland before my amorous neighbor could propose another solution to what she clearly perceived as the predicament of lonely and desperate foreign aid workers.

Imud

T he experience of maturing young boys in the northern
part of Luzon in terms of the relationship between
sexes was not, I would assume, too different from what
it was in other parts of the world. It was played out in various
settings, involved a wide range of ages, and included an array
of rituals and sometimes trickery.

We had in Laoag some believers in the use of *imud*. This
was a concoction that included "secret" ingredients mixed
with coconut oil prepared on Good Friday. When applied to the
skin of a woman, even just a touch of the oil was supposed to
render the victim hopelessly attracted to the man who applied
it! Oh how the young men in the neighborhood wished they
could have a vial of that stuff and carry it always, just in case.
We ached to know what those secret ingredients were, and
where to get them.

Fascination with the *imud* came as we matured, as we
became more observant of happenings in the natural world

around us, and as we listened with fascination to the older boys brag about their exploits—some real and some imagined, I am sure. And, thank goodness, we also had our share of aggressive women who apparently did not need any *imud.* When I compare these to what I think I have observed in contemporary American culture, we did not have in my small hometown a Dr. Ruth, Playboy magazine, adult movies, or PTAs that demanded sex education in the schools. And I do not think that it was ever expected of parents to sit down with us and discuss the mysteries of procreation.

I was in grade six when I finally came face to face with *imud,* tantalizingly bottled and offered for sale by one of the enterprising and somewhat shady characters in my class. Fascinated by all that power that I finally had in my possession, I looked at my female classmates for possible candidates. I even looked at the teacher! Oh, what power, and how I enjoyed considering the prospects! I wavered, however, as I began to wonder whether I really had the energy and stamina equal to the possibilities that were bottled up in my possession. Not willing to give up, I hit upon an idea.

In class I had noticed that Ignacio appeared a bit bored with the lecture. To compound his problems, he was not getting anywhere with Marcelina for whom he had a crush. I did not blame Marcelina. One look at Ignacio would have quickly dispelled any romantic notions on the part of any girl in our class. Ignacio was slightly cross-eyed, a bit on the skinny side, and was barely passing his courses, a condition which did nothing to compensate for his slovenly appearance. But, he was good-natured and was never a discipline problem in class.

During recess, I told Ignacio I had something he might be interested in, but I would have to share it with him secretly. We walked towards the woodworking building and looked around to be sure we were not followed.

I showed him the bottle. After I explained what the content of the bottle was and what it could do, his face lit up more than I had ever seen in class. I told him I would let him try it, and we would wait for the right moment.

We went back to the school ground where most of the students were passing the time under the shade of the *acacia* tree. Ignacio looked around eagerly, and I followed behind until he saw Marcelina, who happened to be by herself, leaning against the fence. Without much ado, Ignacio opened the bottle, put some on his hand, and approached Marcelina unceremoniously. I kept my distance about five yards away, equally eager to witness the power of the *imud*. I could tell that Marcelina was surprised at Ignacio's approach, and looked horrified when he touched her lightly on the elbow. Ignacio stood there briefly, looking at Marcelina, probably expecting her to capitulate then and there. I did not know if the *imud* was that effective. In retrospect, maybe it was potent but not in the way we expected. Marcelina promptly slapped Ignacio on the face and she shouted: "What on earth is that smelly thing you put on my arm?" We vanished quickly into the crowd while Marcelina walked hurriedly over to the faucet to wash.

Did I get a refund for the *imud?* Of course not, but I hope I was a wiser man as a result of pre-testing the substance with the help of Ignacio. I resolved then that I better stick to the old fashion way: a gift of a handkerchief during Christmas, an offer to carry her books on the way home from school, and so on. Serenading at night came later, when we were in the high school.

Many years later as I was working in the front garden of the Segundo house, I could hear a band coming down Rizal Street playing a faintly recognizable and anemic version of a Sousa march. It was a wedding procession where the bride and groom walked at the head of a small group of relatives, a few friends, and some of those people who were always on the lookout for weddings, baptisms, and funerals, whether they were invited or not, so that they could tag along and partake of the free food. As I looked closer, the groom was a beaming Ignacio. The bride was not Marcelina, but I scratched my head, wondering if Ignacio had found an *imud* that had worked after all.

Lovers' Lane

Even though my contemporaries and I grew up in a small town without the conveniences of a car or diverse sources of information like television, magazines, and the internet, we did manage to develop physically, along with its anticipated pleasures with the limited resources at hand. This occurred inevitably in spite of the mores that were intended to restrain us from straying into forbidden territories. Initial sources of information about girls were often older relatives or the other boys in the neighborhood. There was always a lingering doubt about how credible their stories were. Nonetheless, their narrations were always entertaining, and being unable to draw the line between fact and fiction did not really bother us very much. Stories about girls were intensely fascinating to us younger boys even if it was not easy to imagine or visualize what they meant by "seductive smoky fragrance," "velvety skin," "silky hair," "warm sweet breath," etc. In spite of these ambiguities, becoming a man was eagerly anticipated.

"Do you have that catalog again?"

Many opportunities awaited us in our initiation into the world of grown-ups, and we were very receptive. There were no Playboy or Penthouse magazines, but we discovered Sears Roebuck and Montgomery Ward catalogs and the advertisements in their women's section! Mother and Auntie Onor used these catalogs as reference for dress designs they sewed for their customers. They sometimes asked us what we were doing with the catalog. I remember explaining that the guns and toys advertised were interesting!

A different perspective was promised by the older boys of the neighborhood who claimed that peeping under some houses with bamboo floors yielded vistas that were far better than pictures from catalogs. This greatly intrigued me, but I was dubious for a number of reasons. While I could understand the visual possibilities of the *ba-sar* (split bamboo floor) which were laid in strips with open spaces between for ventilation and to facilitate cleaning, I was apprehensive about the risks involved. Sometimes the spaces between the *ba-sar* were conveniently used to drain the *seg-get* (thickened boiling water from cooking rice). And being so close to a floor that was sometimes no more than four or five feet high from the ground, I dreaded the possibility of detection, especially if the people had a dog. But then, the prospects were irresistible. I decided to accompany these boys in their next mission.

A house was selected that had been frequented by the veteran peeping Toms, and they had stories to prove it. I knew the place had residents who were indeed worth the risks for they were young, pretty, and shapely. Because the women of the house usually congregated in the kitchen when food was being prepared for the evening, our mission was to coincide with that time. The four of us, three veterans and one neophyte, waited behind the bushes at the back of the house. One by one, under cover of darkness, we negotiated the distance of about fifty feet from the plants to the space beneath the kitchen, just as we had seen in the movies where the actors attacked an enemy objective. There were three women in the kitchen chatting away as they prepared dinner, and they moved about occasionally. I was surprised to see how light filtered through their dresses! I understood then how the boys came to name one of the women in another house as "Mameng *Bot-bot*" (hole in a garment).

Although the episode was revealing enough, our contortions under the *ba-sar* struck me as ridiculous and comical. I felt like laughing, but succeeded in refraining from doing so. A

Exploring the unknown

dog in the kitchen started to growl. At first, one of the women shushed the dog. At that point I decided it was time to quit, and I quickly retraced my way back to the shrub. The dog then began barking in earnest, and the rest of the boys came running behind me. Probably blamed for provoking the dog, I was cold shouldered by the boys for a few days after that, and never again was I invited for another expedition.

My "education" progressed to other areas. As one of five orderlies in a medical dispensary at a US Air Force base outside Laoag, I was required to assist in handing out little envelopes to the GIs as they boarded the truck for an evening in town. Curious about the envelope, I opened one of them to see what was inside. It was a pair of condoms. I knew what they were for, but there was also a little pouch about four times the size of a teabag. I asked the other orderly what it was for, and he told me it was to put the testicles in to minimize contact. I cannot say whether that was true or not, but I never tested it empirically. I did infer that it was probably a reasonable explanation, judging from the size of the bag. On reflection, the process of getting "all dressed up" for sex with condom, tea bag, etc., seemed much too complicated. But then all these were for a good reason, especially with the problem of venereal disease among the prostitutes patronized by the American soldiers.

The known prostitutes in town were rounded up every other week by the medical section of the air base and brought to the camp by ambulance. The doctor at our dispensary examined them to insure that they were in good health. At the dispensary there were five orderlies. Three younger ones, including me, were told to "get lost" when the prostitutes arrived at the camp. The two older ones stayed to assist the doctor, who was American. I am not a glutton for work, but I thought it was quite unfair, on those occasions, that we were not being given the opportunity to complete an honest day's work!

The high school finally re-opened and it was time to quit work at the air base. I was seventeen, and I was just entering the second year of a four-year high school. Our education had been interrupted by the Second World War. Returning to high school marked another step toward maturity. Going out with girls was then an expected experience, although a few had started earlier. Dating consisted of activities such as going to parties, movies, or escorting a date to a number of our high school programs like the Junior Prom, Senior Prom, Junior-Senior Prom, Military Ball, and Teachers' Ball. Transportation was mostly by walking, for the events were usually held at the high school. If the location was a bit far to walk, four or even six people in a tight squeeze might share the horse-drawn *calesa*. A few might use the bicycle with the girl in back, on the *cargadera* (small sitting platform behind the saddle), or on the bar in front of the cyclist. No one in our class had a car at his or her disposal. School-sponsored programs were usually festive and wholesome for everybody. Simple refreshments like sandwiches, cookies, and punch were served. No alcoholic drinks were allowed.

For dating not related to activities sponsored by the school, students had to be enterprising to overcome problems of venue and transportation. This is where the "tutorials" with the street-corner boys came in handy. The knowledge gained from the mentors of the school of hard knocks was soon to be tested. Transportation depended upon what was available, but that was usually not much of a problem. Venue was more of a challenge, but not insurmountable. I am sure some have fond memories of secluded spots along the *kapanagan* (dry river bed) during the dry season when the sand would have been their only inconvenience. More of a challenge was the monsoon rain. Some people contented themselves with the limited protection afforded by the Gilbert Bridge. More protection from the rain could be sought in the *galyera*, a favorite building of cock-fighting *aficionados* located at the edge of the town. It was used mainly on Sundays, and was open and unguarded at night. While the *nipa* roof provided effective protection from the rain, the smell of chicken dung was not conducive to steamy encounters. Some courageous ones climbed the balcony of the two-story women's dormitory at night, but the rhythmic creaking of that old wooden floor must have been disconcerting indeed!

Three is a crowd.

With great foresight, the elders of the town of Laoag designated a wooded and landscaped patch of land next to the high school as "Lovers' Lane." Unforeseen by our caring founding fathers, however, were the scavenging pigs which also frequented that location and showed absolutely no respect for the privacy of lovers. In the process of looking for food, pigs would actually come right up, snort, grunt, and sometimes even nudge an amorous couple. Perhaps the dish of *lechon,* a whole pig roasted to golden perfection, may be a just retribution for those interrupted early romantic adventures!

lechon

Part III
Beyond Textbooks

Did I Fail Them?

I have sometimes reflected on some decisions I have made in the past, and have wondered whether I should have acted differently. In this chapter, I recall a few instances in which I declined an offer and/or request, and since then I have asked myself if, in turning them down, I have been negligent of my responsibilities as a human being.

One incident took place in Ann Arbor in the 1970s in my pleasant and peaceful neighborhood of single-family dwellings. A house had been recently rented by two men who were perhaps in their thirties, and it was drawing some attention among those who resided in the vicinity because of the unusual amount of traffic of young men that visited the place. Cars would park briefly, and then speed off only to be replaced by others. Sometimes young people went in the house with incongruous-looking containers such as golf bags without golf clubs. The traffic at that house was so heavy that a resident there once told me that I should not park on their side of the street because they "need the space"!

I myself began to have some suspicions about the activities of those neighbors across the street from my house. One day I responded to a knock at our front door. A man in jogging shorts greeted me. He immediately informed me that he was a government agent and he showed me a badge. I do not recall if he was a local or state agent. He asked me if I would be willing to keep track of the activities going on at the house in question. Would I collect information like the number of vehicles, the car licenses, the number of people, how long they stayed, etc.? And could I also take pictures from our window? Remembering how one of the residents had approached me one time to tell me I should not park on their side of the street, I had a feeling that I might be dealing with some unsavory characters, and that it was probably not a good idea to tangle with them.

It occurred to me, too, that if someone from the office of the agent was secretly in touch with the residents of that house, those under surveillance would eventually find out who the informer had been. I politely declined the request. I am sure some more courageous soul took up that responsibility. As it turned out, the authorities eventually raided the house but not until a day or two after the occupants had vacated the place! Were they tipped ahead of time?

Another situation occurred after the publication of *Student Political Activism* (1989), an international reference book that included case studies of the evolution of student activism in different countries. I was the author of the chapter on the Philippines. This chapter started with the history of student activism from the days of the "reformers" during the latter part of the Spanish occupation in the 1890s, and continued with the movement for political independence from the American regime in the 1930s, to the political unrest that marked the administration of Ferdinand Marcos beginning in the 1970s. This was accompanied by an analysis of the variables that facilitated and those that impeded the formation of effective student movements in the Philippines.

I do not know if the article had anything to do with a phone call I received after the publication of the book. The caller identified himself as a member of a federal agency that had something to do with collecting and analyzing data. The man asked if I would be willing to serve as an "analyst" for their agency. He explained that I would help in processing a variety of documents that, I presumed, would be in what they surmised to be my area of expertise. Being unprepared for the offer, I said I would like to give it some thought, since I had recently assumed some additional responsibilities at the university. He left a number that I could call. In about a month, I received another call. It was a woman following up the offer made by the previous caller. Since I had already considered the matter carefully, I declined. As before, she left the same phone number that I could call should I change my mind.

When I was offered work as an "analyst," whatever that meant, I had visions of an assignment that carried an aura of intrigue and adventure. I found that appealing, not to mention the possibility of government-subsidized trips to conferences in the US and, possibly, in the Philippines. I recoiled, however, at the thought of exploiting the confidence of colleagues and friends by making use of data collected from them under false pretenses. I think that was the main sticking point that made me turn down the offer.

A third incident took place while I was visiting the Philippines in 1982. Some background information is in order. According to Onofre Corpuz's *The Philippines* (1965), with the declaration of Manila as a Spanish city on June 3, 1571, "the northward expansion of Islam into Luzon was arrested, and the Moslems were to be contained in Mindanao and Sulu. At the same time, the Spaniards obtained an excellent central base for the colonization of the rest of the archipelago." (Corpuz, p. 25) From that period onward, the task of integrating and/or dominating the Moslem segment within the political system of the Philippines, oftentimes marked by violence, has been a persistent challenge to the Christian-dominated government whether under the Spaniards, Americans, or Filipinos.

Fast forward to the 1960s. According to David Wurfel in *Filipino Politics, Development and Decay* (1988):

> Christian migration to Mindanao continued to escalate in the late 1960s; more than three thousand disembarked every week, seeking land. The government defined all unregistered land as "public," though it may have been regarded as clan land by Moro custom, and thus being parceled out to settlers who satisfied certain requirements. Muslims, long bewildered by the concepts of title deeds, were treated with a heavy hand by Christian law enforcement officers who favored Christian land claimants. Muslims saw land-surveying teams as a part of the conspiracy against their whole way of life and often attacked them. Land conflict was at root a clash of two cultures at different stages of development. (Wurfel, p. 155)

With the escalating violence between Christians and Moslems spawned by this rocky relationship, the Philippine government had to explore new economic and educational programs to deal with Mindanao. It was within this context that, while I was in the Philippines as a recipient of an award from the Philippine government in 1982, I had an invitation to join the Under-secretary of Defense for a private breakfast. One of the fellow honorees happened to be the brother of the Under-secretary and it was through this honoree that the invitation was extended. When I inquired more about the occasion, my fellow honoree said he did not know much about it except that his brother, the Under-secretary, seemed interested that I was getting my award in education. Curious about what the meeting entailed, I agreed to meet the Under-secretary who, according to Wurfel, was then a "Rear Admiral and the highest-ranking Filipino officer in Mindanao." (Wurfel p. 161)

The Under-secretary and I met in one of the restaurants in Manila. He outlined his department's plan to develop an education program to rehabilitate the growing number of Moslem prisoners taken by the Philippine government as a result of the campaign against Moslem insurgency in Mindanao. In that connection, he wondered if I would be willing to serve as a consultant for their project. I thought it was a very interesting and a much-needed program, so I expressed interest and indicated that I wanted to know more about it.

After breakfast we went to his office to go over some related documents. Some of the people in his office brought out brochures and other materials that I scanned as quickly as possible in order to get some sense of what they planned to achieve and what activities they already had in the field. I told the Under-secretary that I was impressed by the department's idea of prisoner rehabilitation, and that I wanted to give some thought to the idea of working in the Philippines if I could obtain a leave of absence from Eastern Michigan University.

I realized many of the Moslem prisoners represented different groups of activists dedicated to causes for which they were apparently willing to risk their lives. One group hoped for more social and economic justice from the Philippine government, another for greater political autonomy, and the most radical bunch wanted a complete separation from the Philippine Republic. I am sure there were also those who were probably nothing more than bandits who were taking advantage of the civil unrest. With such high stakes involved, I fully realized that getting involved as consultant to such a project was a dangerous undertaking that tolerated no room for sophomoric or utopian thinking.

I discussed with my father what had transpired at my meeting with the Under-secretary of Defense, and I later contacted a long-time friend (from kindergarten days!) who was then a high-ranking officer in an "Intelligence Section" of the Philippine Army. I wanted my friend's thinking about a number of things, including the reputation of the Defense department among the Moslems, the status of the government's education project, and the problems of security in Mindanao. To make a long story short, I was informed that the image of the Defense department among the Moslems was not good, and that included the reputation of some of the Moslems working in high positions within the government. I understood from my friend, therefore, that working in Mindanao as a consultant for the Department would be very risky indeed, and I would not be an effective consultant if I limited my work location to Manila. The advice was clear: "Don't get involved; it's not good for your health!"

If I consider what I read today in the papers about the continuing unrest in Mindanao—gun battles, kidnappings, assassinations, and even executions—I can say that the advice of my good friend was very sound indeed. I listened to him, and that determined my response when I eventually turned down this chance to participate in what I initially thought was a promising program.

Another quandary had to do with a former high school student who was in one of my courses. The student was quiet in class, never disruptive, but a poor achiever. Sometimes I paid extra attention to such students for I thought they need more help than the noisy ones. The father sometimes dropped by to chat before I left for the day. He became a good friend, and we chatted about a number of things. He also expressed concern about his son who was doing poorly in my class. I extended what help I could to the boy. He barely passed the course, and that was the last time I heard about him until five years later when, in the local paper, there was an item on vandalism of parked cars in a certain neighborhood. One of those arrested was my former student. A year later, the young man was in the local paper again for breaking and entering. To me the signs were not encouraging. It looked like he was a candidate for bigger problems. I was saddened by the realization that the life of a former student was unfolding in a very negative way. I remembered, too, my after-class conversations with his father.

Years passed since I taught in the high school, and many professional and family changes in my life had transpired. My two daughters were already in the elementary grades. One evening, I received a telephone call from the father of that same former student who had problems with the law. Needless to say, the call was a surprise to me. The main reason for the father's call was that his son wanted me to get in touch with him (the son) since he was back in prison. It was a strange message, but I pursued the conversation. I was informed that the son was imprisoned for battery and attempted murder. The father left a phone number and instructions on how I could get in touch with an inmate at that state prison.

Maybe I had made a positive impression on my former student, but then what could I do for him years later? As I gave more thought to the matter, there was a news item in the local paper about a young social worker who had occasionally offered her apartment for an overnight stay for some of her out-of-town clients. They had just discovered her body, murdered presumably by one of her guests! That greatly influenced my decision about whether or not I should contact my former student who was in prison. What, I thought, would I do if the prisoner were out one day and wanted a place to stay for the night? The probability of that happening was small indeed, and I could have declined. But with my young family, why take a chance? Based on that, I decided to ignore the request to contact my former student.

Unfortunately, memories of events such as these cannot be easily relegated to the past to be forgotten completely. These voices have a way of coming back whether we like it or not, forcing us to take an accounting once in a while of how we conduct our lives and how we relate to other people. If anything can come out of it, I hope reflections such as these about the past make us more sensitive to the consequences of the decisions we make and how they affects us and other people.

Language Barriers

L anguage must be one of the most important inventions of mankind. It allows us to accomplish so many complex and useful things, and yet it is available to everybody. With language we communicate thoughts, convey feelings, provide a framework for solving difficult problems and, when we write, language helps both to make and to preserve history. In short, it is reasonable to say that language has made human society possible. And yet given its complexity and its uses to society, learning a language is a birthright of everybody, and without cost!

For all the blessings that language has brought to our society, it can also subject us to many things we can do without. I certainly do not have much use, for instance, for telemarketers, rap music, sound bites, advertisements that interrupt my favorite programs, or listening to politicians who I suspect of calculated misrepresentations to mislead the public.

Another perversion of language, in my opinion, is what appears as the propensity of some folks in our region in the Philippines for "baptizing" people based on some physical deformity, handicap, or personal habit. A few examples come to mind. Someone was nicknamed *Kimmot ti Manok* (rectum of the chicken) for the unfortunate configuration of his mouth which tended to resemble that part of the chicken's anatomy. There was that severe-looking fellow in Laoag with a thick moustache who was nicknamed *Infierno*. Why? I do not clearly recall except that he did look like someone who harbored some dark secrets! Other common nicknames based on physical handicaps were *Pilay* (lame), *Singkol* (elbow with an abnormal angle), *Gosing* (harelip), *Pangkis* (cross-eyed), *Sol-ot* (deaf), *Iep-ped* (flat nose), *Burtong* (small pox), and so on.

Our teachers had their nicknames, too. The woman who taught the Philippine National Language, *Tagalog*, was appropriately nicknamed Miss *Pantukoy* (an article in Tagalog grammar). Our horticulture teacher was regarded highly for his command of the subject, but for some reason he always referred to the common banana as *Musa Sapientum*. The fruit was a regular item on many Filipino tables, hence, it was amusing to hear it referred to frequently with such an alien name. You guessed it. Our horticulture teacher soon earned the distinguished sobriquet of *Musa Sapientum*! Ask any surviving member of that horticulture class, and they would surely remember *Musa*, and not by any other name!

Personal appearance did not escape the name givers. I have never figured out why one fellow was named *Doguiot* (untidy) when, as I remember him, he was usually neat. The name stuck, and the poor man was always referred to as *Doguiot*. And beware of quirky personality traits for that was fair game, too. One woman was named *Moriot* (crybaby) for being so moody.

One case of behavior leading to a nickname was that of the self-appointed dispenser of news during the war. He shared his information with people in the neighborhood about the progress of the Americans in the Pacific as they fought their way towards the Philippines. He claimed to have a shortwave radio, an item that was forbidden by the Japanese, so our "newsman" enjoyed the center stage, so to speak, when he was among friends as he whispered the "latest development." Some people were not so impressed, however, and nicknamed him *Biki Biki* (probably an onomatopoetic derivation of being talkative). I remember Mother complained about *Biki Biki* when he delayed mealtime as Father politely listened to him at the street corner near the house.

On another occasion while *Biki Biki* held forth and *Tio* Deriong (brother of Mother) was the hapless listener, a dog came around, got close to the two people, sniffed *Biki Biki's* pants, and urinated on *Biki Biki's* pant leg. I do not know if you can call that a canine editorial comment, but it seemed like *Biki Biki* got a bladder-full before he noticed what had happened. Whether or not that dampened *Biki Biki's* account of the war was hard to tell.

I can say that the listeners of *Umel* (deaf-mute) were more appreciative than the audience of *Biki Biki*. What her real name was, I never knew, but everyone within the vicinity called the tiny and spunky woman *Umel*. Her forte was the juiciest gossip. She was quite descriptive with her gestures and could

Canine reaction to Biki Biki

very effectively convey whatever were the current intimate and forbidden liaisons in the neighborhood. Not surprisingly, the other women, even those who were supposed to be respectable, would surround this little woman and they would burst into laughter with *Umel*'s graphic hand gestures account of the latest episode.

Regardless of what we want or do not want to hear, language can sometimes reveal where we are from, our ethnic background (if we cannot shake off that accent), even our social class for those who think they can discern such things. When teaching in the United States, I tried to anticipate any criticisms by announcing at the beginning of each semester that if the students wondered what my accent was, it was "a Filipino accent complicated by decades of living in Michigan." In other words, I tried to convey to my students that I was aware I had a different accent from what they were used to, and that it was something I regarded with humor and nothing more. Consequently, if I stumbled over some words, it was for me simply an occasion for humor, not awkwardness. Not being able to distinguish the subtle differences in the pronunciation of some words, I confessed I was hopelessly mixing up the pronunciation of words like "itch," "each," "its," and "eats." And I told them, too, about the surprised look on a waitress when I ordered what sounded like "soap" instead of "soup"! So to the students, when I had one of those mix-ups, it was just a little detour to liven things up, and we moved on after any needed clarifications.

Sometimes my accent has come in handy, however, and I have made use of it accordingly. When I have participated at conferences of the Comparative and International Education Society, I have sometimes emphasized my Filipino accent to add credibility to my presentation about the Philippines. It might even have discouraged some non-Filipinos from questioning the veracity of what I was saying! When some organizations in Michigan invited me to speak on the Philippines, I am sure they were assuming that I must be an expert on that country. If only they had realized that I have lived in the US longer than I have in the Philippines, and that I had to run to the library, like everyone else, to research what I was going to talk about. But when my talk is delivered with that accent, I guess it sounds very authentic for everybody, especially when I wear my *Barong*, that handsome Filipino shirt, for added effect.

How wonderful it is that through language we can build bridges across cultures. My daughter, Cindy, has always been proud of her heritage from both sides of her family. She visited the Philippines with our family when she was still preschool age. She also opted, when she was older, to miss a semester of college in the United States so that she could spend a little more time with *Lola* and *Lolo* in the Philippines. In situations like these where one is visiting a different country as a guest, one often begins to pick up words here and there, and even tries to form a sentence or two, to the delight of the hosts. One time in the Philippines while the family was having the afternoon *merienda* (tea time), Cindy tried one of her newly learned words. She asked if someone could pass the steamed bread. Instead of saying *puto,* however, she requested the *puta* (whore)! The laughter at the table was good-natured, of course, and Cindy had just as good a laugh as the others. She might have felt a little embarrassed then, but she surely earned some brownie points for at least trying!

Although learning a language nearly guarantees that we will have awkward and embarrassing moments, I have found ways to capitalize on this fact. While researching a paper when I was a graduate student, I decided to go to the Newberry Library in Chicago where they had a good collection of materials about the Philippines. From the Chicago Loop, I decided to walk because I was told it was "only a few blocks down in that direction." It turned out to be a rather long walk, and I noticed that the neighborhood I went through did not look safe for strangers like me. Thus, after I finished my research at the library and it was getting to be late in the afternoon, I thought I should take the bus back to the Loop. While waiting at the bus stop by myself, I was approached by a young lady. She asked if I would like to have a "good time." Uh, oh, I thought. She was nice-looking and dressed for an evening out. I did not want to be unpleasant to her. After searching for a quick response, I finally came up with a polite bow and said, "Solee. No speakee!" "What are you doing in this country if you cannot speak English?" was her annoyed response. She stomped, and turned away in apparent disgust. Still I could not help but admire her swaying hips as she walked away.

"What are you doing in this country if you cannot speak English!"

Pruning The Family Tree

y usually mild-mannered and gentle Uncle Larry, in Chicago, was quite agitated and even mumbled a few expletives. That caught my attention. I asked him if there was anything wrong. He said he had just read his mail, a letter from the Philippines that he had been eagerly awaiting to verify his date of birth for Social Security requirements. Now he finally had a copy of a church document that listed his date of birth. "So what is the problem?" I inquired. He was quiet for a while and did not seem inclined to explain. But I was curious, and persisted. When he finally responded, he said the document had listed him as "illegitimate." He repeated the term with disgust. I did not know what to make out of it, but I felt sympathy for Uncle Larry for he was always proud of his family.

After a careful review in my mind of what I remembered about Philippine history, I found a possible explanation, and I shared it with him a few days later. I theorized that since it was a church document and that Lola and Lolo's marriage may have been solemnized in a civil court, the church did not recognize the marriage as valid. Thus, consistent with the arrogance of the Roman Catholic Church that expounded on its supremacy over civil authorities, was the classification of children born under a civil union as illegitimate or born out of wedlock! I think that pacified him somewhat, but the initial reaction of Uncle Larry reflected the stigma that the people in our town of Laoag felt about the status of illegitimate children, those who were born out of wedlock. There was even a special term that was used for the pregnancy of an unmarried woman: *nadesgracia* (disgraced). Accordingly, some families resorted to creative ways to conceal what they regarded as a stain on their status or reputation in the community. The offspring of an amorous son, for instance, with a housemaid or with the daughter of a tenant farmer could very well be hidden away in some obscure location. If it was an unmarried daughter, and marriage with the offending buck was not possible or not approved by the girl's family, she was likely banished suddenly, sent to spend time with a relative somewhere.

When I was in the process of writing my book, *At the Table With the Family*, it occurred to me to include a family tree. I was stymied when I encountered a wall of secrecy about the illegitimate children of grandparents, uncles, cousins, nephews, etc. Consequently, I was able to include only an "abbreviated" version of our family tree.

The issue of illegitimacy in my province of Ilocos Norte has not always been clear cut. Common-law arrangements were sometimes widespread in earlier periods. Sometimes peasants far from urban centers where the church and courts were located found it inconvenient to travel to solemnize a relationship. Or some couples may not have had any money to go through the church or civil requirements followed by the expected celebrations of food and drinks.

From my own perspective, even those born out of wedlock are members of our biological family, whether we like it not. The issue has evoked for me humorous and amusing memories, rather than recollections that I was ashamed of. It is the concealment and denial that I find shameful. My regret, therefore, is in not knowing more about all my illegitimate relatives who are classified as such by hypocritical social conventions. I recognize that there might be issues of inheritance that make this matter of legitimacy a touchy subject for some families. But how I would have loved to share stories with all my relatives, share our happiness, and also our dreams. I can remember a few stories and here are a couple of them:

Once, as recounted in *At the Table with the Family*, when I was still of preschool age and played in front of the Segundo house, I waited for my *Lolo* Nicolas to come home from his law practice. I could always recognize him for he was always in a white suit with a black tie, a stiff-brimmed hat, and a cane that he swung in a particular way. I was always glad to see him. I would run to meet him and we would walk up the path together.

Finally, there he was. I ran to meet him as I always did, but I was taken aback for, although he looked an awful lot like *Lolo* and had the same outfit, he looked younger. I did not reach for his hand, as I usually did with *Lolo*. Instead, I ran back to the house to tell Mother about the strange experience. She smiled, and she did not say anything. It was that secrecy thing again.

I learned later that the man I saw was the illegitimate son of *Lolo* Nicolas, the fruit of his clandestine visits to his girlfriend when he was a seminary student preparing to become a priest of the Roman Catholic Church. He was counseled to consider other professions when his "extra-curricular activities" were eventually discovered.

On a different occasion two veiled women sat in the *sala* of the Samonte house in front of a puzzled gentleman in his eighties. The women were quietly reminding him that he had forgotten them, that this was his daughter, and that they have not been getting their share of the rice harvest. Poor *Lolo* Justo! What was he suppose to make out of all this? He looked bewildered, according to Mother. Because his eyesight was failing, he squinted hard, trying to recognize the two mysterious women behind the veils. As it turned out, it was a prank orchestrated by *Lola* Sabina, his wife, with the cooperation of two daughters-in-law, Mother, and Auntie Onor, the wife of Uncle Vicente. When *Mama* Ti, the eldest daughter of *Lola* and *Lolo*, heard about this, she scolded all the actors, including the producer, for playing such a cruel joke on poor *Lolo*.

Let me get back to my aborted attempt to include a more complete family tree in my book. How nice it would have been to see a family tree in full bloom, not one that was mercilessly pruned just to maintain a facade of respectability. But if there is any truth to all I have heard about the travels and adventures of my elders, I realize it would be quite a challenge indeed to construct one with so many branches. Nonetheless, we can imagine what a magnificent tree that would be!

"Have you forgotten us?"

First Impressions

I was pleasantly surprised when a colleague who asked me out to lunch inquired if I would serve as interim assistant dean of the graduate school of Eastern Michigan University. Although that colleague was neither an administrator nor in a position of power in the university, I sensed that he was probably asked to test my reaction, since we were good friends. Not prepared for the question, I responded that it was an interesting idea and I would have to give it some thought.

I have never entertained any ambition of becoming a university administrator. I enjoyed teaching because of its flexible schedule, opportunity to debate issues with students, and the chance it affords to participate professionally abroad. On the other hand, I thought it might be a good experience to find out how an administrator functions and to have a better idea about how it feels to be on the other side of the fence, so to speak, vis-à-vis the faculty. The possibility that I could be involved in helping shape policy in the graduate school was also appealing.

When my colleague came to see me again a couple of days later, he told me that the dean of the College of Education had asked him to check how I reacted to the idea of my serving as interim assistant dean. He suggested I should see the dean to find out more about it if I was interested.

I decided that it would not be a bad idea to explore the matter, and I made an appointment to see the dean. The dean gave me some background information about why an interim dean and assistant dean were needed in the graduate school. It appeared that there were some serious violations of North Central Association's (NCA) accreditation standards, and that Eastern Michigan University needed to do some house cleaning, and quickly. There was an issue about a master's degree program that was never authorized by the NCA, but was being offered by the dean of the graduate school, and that academic departments had complained loudly that the unauthorized degree was being used as a way for the graduate school to bypass departmental requirements to a degree program.

Since I have a tendency to respond to a challenge instead of backing away from it, I told the dean I was willing to give it a try. I added, however, that I did not have any administrative experience. He assured me that the interim dean and I would have a lot of flexibility in proposing some badly needed reforms. He added that the interim dean would be the then-current dean of the College of Business who had a reputation as a no-nonsense administrator. What followed was an interview with the vice-president of instruction, who briefed me about the situation in the graduate school. To make a long story short, that is how I found myself as interim assistant dean of the graduate school of Eastern Michigan University at the beginning of the school year 1969.

The first day in my new assignment involved the usual round of meeting with the interim dean, the administrative assistant, and the dozen or so members of the secretarial staff. I was also introduced to one who was designated as my secretary! I made a mental note that the secretaries were young and nice-looking, and that the one assigned to me was the best looking of them all. First day on the job was not, I thought, the time to burden my mind with serious matters like reforming the graduate school. There would be time enough for that later on. I must first take stock of the ambience of the setting. Not bad, I thought.

There were many things to do, and I was given to understand that we had a great deal of leeway to initiate changes. The previous dean had opted for early retirement, and his assistant dean had returned to his faculty position. With the encouragement of the interim dean, whom I met every morning before the beginning of each workday, I proposed that we should first repair relationships with the academic departments and codify all existing policies in the graduate school. This was because there seemed to be no clear-cut understanding of some policies on the part of the faculty, the secretaries, and the students. There was a need, too, for the secretaries to have a clearer division of labor so that each group could develop an area of expertise and be assigned specific academic departments to deal with. A lot of things to do, I thought, but it was exciting and I looked forward to my new job.

I suggested to the administrative assistant that I wanted a

meeting with all the secretaries so that I could impart a better understanding of (1) why the dean and I were assigned to the graduate school, (2) what we intended to do, how, and why, (3) what we expected from the secretaries, and (4) what they could expect from us to support them in their work. It would also be an opportunity for them to ask any initial questions concerning the transition period. The administrative assistant thought that was a great idea. He asked when he could assemble them for the meeting. I suggested I preferred to meet each one individually first, and visit each one at her table. A general meeting would be good, I said, at a later date. So it was planned accordingly.

On the day I was scheduled to visit each secretary I put on my good dark-gray suit. I was intent on projecting an image of a well-groomed administrator, a good "listener," and all that sort of thing. Right before I made the rounds, I went to the restroom to be sure I looked presentable.

Since the main secretarial office was a fairly huge room, probably equivalent to two classrooms combined, the secretarial tables were organized with a bit of space between them. All my quiet talk with each secretary could be conducted without, I assumed, the person at the next table overhearing the conversation. From the neatness of the desks, it looked as if the secretaries had prepared for the occasion, too. I approached each table, stood in front of it, and engaged in the small talk necessary to ascertain how long the secretary had been on the job, how she liked it, any problems with parking on the campus, was she taking courses, and so on. It took about ten to fifteen minutes to visit each one. It was too short a visit to actually

"Did I make a good first impression?"

cover anything of substance, but it was essentially a symbolic gesture to dramatize my interest in what each of them did.

Having completed the visits, I went to see the administrative assistant, and stood in front of his desk just as I had done with each of the secretaries. I informed him that I thought the whole thing had gone very well. He leaned back, puffed on his pipe, and listened. He commented that they were good secretaries, but that they had been working under rather stressful conditions without a division of labor, not to mention dealing with complaints from students and from the faculty. He puffed at his pipe some more, which created quite a bit of smoke that partially obscured his face. He waved his hand, clearing the smoke. Then he said, "Your fly is open!" At first I was bewildered by the comment. This man has a strange sense of humor, I thought, or was that some kind of a profound metaphor for something? But I looked down, nonetheless, just to check, and sure enough, it was open! I sat down on the chair in front of his table. A flood of questions flashed through my mind: How could I have done such a careless thing? What did the secretaries think? How would I face them again?

I remembered my visit to the restroom before I met the secretaries. I was sure that I had pulled my zipper up. That, too, I remembered. But I was not aware that the closing mechanism had not attached to the other side of the zipper! Oh well. It had been with the best of intentions that I had wanted to be presentable, but not in this way. As it turned out, thankfully, my tenure in the graduate school was blessed with very pleasant, attractive, and dependable secretaries who were also, I think, very understanding. I like to believe that my introduction to the secretaries did not affect the quality of my work during my time there. If it is any measure of my performance as interim assistant dean, I was asked by the vice president for Academic Affairs to stay on in the graduate school with the starting rank of Associate Dean of the Graduate School. It was a difficult offer to turn down, but the call of teaching and debating students was more compelling for me. Reluctantly, I turned down the possibility of becoming a university administrator permanently.

Back to the fiasco with the open fly. If misery loves company, I found some consolation in a story related by one of my colleagues. He had been giving a presentation in one of the small auditoriums of the university which had a seating capacity of about two hundred. Since my colleague was giving a special lecture, several sections of a few classes attended. The stage did not have any furniture except for an upright piano that was close to the center. My colleague, as he usually did, was moving around while giving his talk. He paced and gestured now and then to emphasize a point. As he told me later, he happened to look down and he noticed that his fly was open. Without missing a beat, he continued talking and walked casually towards the back of the piano. According to him, he managed to pull his zipper up without interrupting his pace and his lecture. He emerged at the other side of the piano thinking that he had unobtrusively solved his embarrassing problem, when suddenly the students laughed and clapped heartily! With that, he bowed slightly and continued his lecture.

Reception By The US Ambassador

O n the morning of the second day after my arrival in
North Yemen, the education officer of the United
States Agency for International Development (USAID)
called my office. He informed me that the United States ambassador to the Yemen Arab Republic wanted to see me. I was
at the time in North Yemen to assume my duties as "Chief of
Party" of an education project funded by the USAID and sub-
contracted by Eastern Michigan University (EMU). Surprised
by the prompt invitation, I inquired if this was a reception for
new arrivals. "Not exactly, he wants to see only you and me," he
responded. I was surprised, and I reflected that I had not realized how important a job I had, that the US ambassador even
knew about my arrival, and that he wanted to see me in person!
I was even more taken aback when the education officer said
the ambassador wanted to meet me right away, and would I be
ready in about an hour?

The education officer picked me up, and we drove through Sanaa to a compound surrounded by a high wall. We entered through a substantial metal gate guarded by two US Marines who checked our US ID cards before we proceeded into a courtyard. I assumed that that was the US embassy with the guards and the American flag on display from a pole in the courtyard. The education officer confirmed that we were already at the embassy. We showed our ID again to another marine before we entered the building. At the reception desk the secretary informed us that the ambassador was expecting us. All these rituals certainly impressed me, but I conducted myself as if this was just in a day's work. I made sure, for instance, that I did not look like a lost soul with my mouth open. We followed the secretary into what looked like a large living room. She asked if she could bring us something to drink, then disappeared.

The ambassador came out immediately and was quite cordial. Starting with the usual pleasantries, he inquired if I had had a good flight, which route I had taken (whether through London or Frankfurt), and if my apartment was in good shape. He even asked where I had gotten my tweed hat, which I had recently bought at Marx and Spencer in London. With pleasantries over, he got down to business. He took off his gloves, so to speak.

He started by declaring that he was highly disturbed and disappointed with the performance of Eastern Michigan University as a subcontractor for USAID. He enumerated some problems, such as work plans that were turning out to be unrealistic and unmanageable, schedules that were not being met, and assignment of some field personnel who were apparently not prepared for their responsibilities. And all these, he added, for a multi-million-dollar project! The ambassador was very angry indeed. After all, he was talking about one of the biggest US foreign aid projects in North Yemen at that time. He went on with his litany of criticisms for what seemed like an hour or so. And he concluded by saying that he thought the university was unprepared to take on a responsibility of that magnitude. He had a comment that stuck with me to the effect that EMU was "a disgrace to higher education."

I listened carefully. Although I was taken aback by the bluntness, I was not intimidated at all for I was familiar with a recently published external evaluation that was highly critical of the manner in which the project was implemented. I assumed that that was probably the basis for the ambassador's comments. As a matter of fact, I had read that evaluation carefully before making up my mind about applying for the job. I think I viewed the project the same way as the ambassador.

Then he turned to me directly and asked pointedly, "What do you plan to do?" I thanked the ambassador for taking the time to meet us, and for his interest in the project. I added that I planned to use the external evaluation as a basis for reviewing the project, and for proposing needed changes. I emphasized that the problem was a complicated one, and I would need all the support he could offer from the field to help me persuade the university to support the changes that should be undertaken. I concluded I was very encouraged, therefore, by the concerns expressed by the ambassador and by the support of the USAID office in Yemen. I do not know if my response pacified the ambassador who was obviously agitated when he assessed the project. We ended our meeting which had lasted for over an hour.

The external evaluation of the project was an incisive and unforgiving documentation of the performance of EMU in undertaking the North Yemen project. I believe that evaluation contributed to shortening the duration of that contract. The US government decided to withhold the unused eighteen million dollars from a twenty-eight-million-dollar project. The reputation of the project was so bad that the president of EMU had even discouraged me from applying. He said that many people associated with the Yemen project had been tainted professionally, so why get involved? I responded that as long as he was aware, on the basis of the external evaluation, that the project was already in bad shape, at least I would not be blamed for the mess it was in. I also asked if I could contact him directly when I was in the field since I thought the Office of International Education on the campus was probably part of the problem. He said I could do that. He added, however, that since he was sometimes away from the campus, perhaps it would be better for me to contact the Associate Vice President of Academic Affairs directly when I needed something of importance from the university while I was in the field.

Suffice it to say that I found it necessary to (1) have a thorough audit of the project in the field to establish a new baseline for its assets and liabilities, (2) reduce the size of the field personnel on the level of team leaders for the sub-projects, and (3) rewrite the work plans to a more manageable proportion. In this connection I must not forget the indispensable support provided for the EMU field team by a no-nonsense, accessible, and able EMU administrator. Dr. Donald H. Bennion, who was then Associate Vice President for Academic Affairs of the university, was my main contact on campus, bypassing what I regarded as a useless university office of international education. Dr. Bennion was decisive and effective in cutting through red tape within the university to enable the field team to overcome the ever-tightening deadlines. Without Dr. Bennion's assistance, I am positive completing the project in a successful manner within the tight time limit designated by the government of North Yemen would not have been possible.

I can say that the project ended well. As I recalled in my other book, *At the Table with the Family,* the prime minister of North Yemen formally opened the completed project, and invited as guests were members of the diplomatic corps including the US ambassador. This was a different ambassador from the one who "welcomed" me to Yemen with a litany of concerns about EMU and the project. The new US ambassador was obviously very pleased with the outcome.

Jambiya, a gift from Sanaa University, North Yemen.

Fine-Tuning Policies

As if negotiating through the maze of federal regulations governing foreign aid was not complicated enough, I also had to contend with the policies and politics of the client countries during my various assignments abroad. And that was not all. Each project field team had a mixture of different levels of competence, which was also true of our counterparts from the client country. On the face of it, government international projects are Gordian knots. With a bit of resourcefulness, however, they can be rendered manageable, and I can honestly say that I thoroughly enjoyed my assignments overseas.

In the 1970s and 1980s, Eastern Michigan University was a subcontractor for the USAID in a number of overseas projects. I was fortunate to have been able participate in two of them, one in Swaziland and the other in North Yemen. One of my introductions to the realities of foreign aid programs was when my wife, Judy, and I attended the required orientation at the Department of State in Washington, DC. In no uncertain terms, one of the lecturers emphasized that foreign aid was not to be equated with American generosity, not a giveaway of resources with no strings attached. This was necessary, he pointed out, to get the funding from tax dollars appropriated by the United States Congress.

Under this arrangement, most of the money in a foreign aid package would eventually come back to the United States. I hope, however, that the United States government will come to regard as abusive and unacceptable situations such as that of Halliburton, if indeed the allegations are true that that company raked in millions of American foreign aid money in the name of "helping" rebuild Iraq. The situation is being investigated, as of this writing.

That foreign aid is motivated mainly by the national self-interest of a donor country was not completely a surprise to me. I have always suspected as much, especially when I reviewed American colonial and post-colonial policies in the Philippines. But the policy looked a bit different when viewed in terms of nuts and bolts by one who was going to help carry out such a policy in microcosm. As the translation of this policy began to unfold at the orientation, it meant, for example, that (1) only American carriers could be used, if available, to transport personnel and necessary materials, (2) salaries of US technicians were to be paid out of the grant for a project, (3) equipment installed overseas must come from the US, as long as adaptive changes were minor enough, like use of electric transformers, (4) American vehicles must be used for the project in the field even if the cost of transportation, maintenance, and insurance was relatively high, (5) scholarships for client countries were designed for American universities even if there were questions as to whether the institutions involved had the appropriate programs or faculty needed for such a responsibility, and (6) most of the furniture for the houses in one project in which I participated came from the United States.

Obviously, these regulations made the projects more expensive, less efficient (when parts for equipment had to come from the United States), and less effective (when scholars from the client country who came to the United States went back home with skills that were hardly useable to their country). I was told about a person from a client country who was trained in the US as an air force pilot. He was eventually assigned to the Ministry of Foreign Affairs stamping passports since his country did not have an air force!

The following are illustrations of adaptations that I resorted to in the field to keep my project going and still be within the policies and regulations of the donor and client countries. Some cases were fairly clear cut, while other decisions I made were more arbitrary. It was not long, for example, before three out of our seven American project cars were in need of parts not available in the client country. Ordering car parts from the United States was out of the question because we did not have time to wait for them and still complete the project within the time limit imposed by North Yemen. I suggested we use the good parts of the three cars to keep the other four going. That provided us with enough vehicles for our transportation until the closing of the project.

Another situation that required some adjustments in procedures was the problem of getting papers approved for the release of essential shipments from the airport and/or harbor. Ordinarily, such a process involved a nightmare of red tape and delay—even packages for the USAID office were not spared from this problem. I did not have time for this sort of delay, and I put effort in finding a "fixer" who knew his way around the red tape and could get our packages through. We usually waited only a day or two after arrival, and had to obtain a minimum of signatures and government stamps! He was my secret weapon, but apparently not too secret for the USAID office later requested if they could "borrow" him for just a short while!

Getting field initiatives off the ground was not always easy if, for example, you had a coworker who, for one reason or another, might block or delay. Capitalizing on my "third world" origins was very helpful indeed, especially when my counterparts from the client country related to me as such. A few informal get-togethers with the right person in the ministry (e.g., over a cup of tea or something stronger, or chewing *qat*, or being invited alone to their homes for dinner) made a lot of difference. This was certainly more effective than relying mainly on writing memos to the Ministry, as I noted from the paper trail left behind by my predecessors in the project.

Dealing with a counterpart from the client country concerning an issue he might feel strongly about was something else. I had to assess each situation carefully. Was the position taken one that officially represented the Ministry, hence, probably non-negotiable? Or was it just a personal opinion of an official whose backing from the Ministry was doubtful? All these had to be balanced carefully with, for example, the donor's interest as well as the integrity of the project. In one situation recounted in my other book, *At the Table with the Family*, the Director of Education, my counterpart, suggested that I fire my American administrative assistant based on the suspicion of the director that my assistant was a Jewish spy for Israel. My response was not a difficult one to decide. The accusation was baseless, presumption of innocence was ignored, and I did not think the position of that official represented that of the Ministry. Although he threatened to terminate the project, I supported my assistant with the backing of the USAID office. The Ministry official backed down, claiming that he was misunderstood. Allowing him room to "save face," I closed the matter at that point. We continued to be good friends, incidentally, and worked well together to complete the project.

The closing of each project required taking stock of the remaining assets that belonged to the United States government. That enabled the project to have a proper accounting of what was under its responsibility and what would be transferred eventually to the Ministry of Education of the client government, the department we worked with. This required removing from our office all US-owned furniture and equipment to a US storage facility for temporary safekeeping until they were formally handed over to the Ministry of Education. When my workers started to move the furniture out of the government building that we occupied with another Ministry that had nothing to do with our project, the employees of that Ministry stopped us. Obviously they wanted the items for themselves. Although I strongly protested that those items belonged to the US government until they were formally handed over to the Ministry of Education, I knew I was not getting anywhere.

At noon the building was empty because everyone went out for lunch. It was a good time, I thought, to move the furniture out of the building. There were desks, long tables, chairs, coffee tables, typewriters, and filing cabinets. But when I suggested to my employees that we could take them all out before the other people came back, I was told an armed guard was posted at the gate! I asked my driver to bring the guard to my office. The driver looked puzzled. He asked what I had in mind. At any rate, the guard came to my office. I greeted the guard. Through my driver as translator, I thanked the guard for coming to the office. I asked what his monthly salary was. I do not remember how much it was exactly, but I figured then that it was a ridiculously small amount. I told him I would double it. His eyes lit up and he asked me what I wanted him to do. I informed him that I wanted to have our office furniture out of the building so that it could be stored properly somewhere. "No problem," he said. He even offered to help carry the items out, but I told him he could go out and have a long lunch. I did not want to incriminate him further.

By the time the other people got back to the building, our office was empty. I was happy, the guard was more than happy, and my employees and I went out to celebrate with a good lunch. I do not know what the other occupants of the building thought when they returned. At least I had cleaned the space for them!

Not By The Book!

Fred, an American employee of the Yemen project, was due to arrive at the international airport in Yemen after a month of vacation in the United States. Although he was scheduled to be at the airport at two o'clock in the morning, he did not arrive until some ten hours later. Delays in departures and arrivals are common enough, and passengers are pretty much at the mercy of the airlines.

Fred finally showed up at the office after lunch. I had never met him. He was a remaining member of a previous team from before my tenure as Chief of Party for the Yemen project. Although he appeared glad that the long trip was over, there was something in our initial talk that made me wonder if he was at all keen about being back with the project. For someone who had just returned from an extended vacation, and was meeting the new Chief of Party for the first time, he certainly did not exhibit much enthusiasm or curiosity about the project. I rationalized that maybe he was just tired. We continued our talk, and my doubts lingered.

The phone rang, and the secretary said it was for me. It was a long distance call from the United States. The caller identified herself as a relative of Fred. She wanted to know if he had arrived. I assured the caller that Fred had arrived safely, and I would soon drive him to his apartment when the office closed for the day. I was not quite prepared, however, when the caller said that she was extremely worried about Fred's return to Yemen. She also mentioned that he had not rested enough and he did not feel like returning to Yemen. She added that "he should not be left alone." What was I supposed to make of that warning, and should I do anything about it? I thanked her for the information and concluded our conversation. I sat in my office alone briefly and tried to make sense of the message. Meanwhile, Fred was sitting by himself in the other room.

After about ten minutes, I joined Fred who was then flipping through the pages of a magazine from the coffee table. We engaged in bit of small talk while my mind was working full speed, evaluating the situation. For one thing, I would find some ways to be with Fred as long as possible.

Fred said, "I feel very tired." Then he mentioned that he would like to have an appointment with the embassy doctor before reporting for regular work. I encouraged him to arrange this visit right away just in case the doctor leaves for one of his field trips. He agreed, and the secretary made the call for Fred at his request. The appointment was set for the following morning.

But what was I to do with Fred until the following day? To begin with, it was easy enough to invite him out to a restaurant for dinner. So, before we took him to his apartment, the driver loaded his luggage in the car and the three of us went to a restaurant. It was an extended dinner indeed, but my dilemma was not over. We discussed how he would react if the doctor suggested that he should return to the US for additional "rest." Needless to say, I was relived to hear when he said that he would gladly abide by whatever the doctor suggested. He lamented the fact, however, that we could not purchase any alcoholic drink at the restaurant. He wondered if we could get any drink anywhere. I mentioned that I had some drinks at the apartment, but I asked him if he was on any medication that might interact adversely with alcohol. He assured me that he was not. Since Fred and I were in the same compound, it was easy enough to drive back, stop at my place, and have our drink. Luggage would be dealt with later, as his apartment was only a few doors down.

We arrived at my apartment around ten in the evening. I went to my room, pulled a box from under my bed, took out an unopened bottle of *Fundador,* a Spanish brandy that the US commissary sold to members of the US embassy staff and those affiliated with the USAID program. I made sure I got my monthly quota of wine, beer, and brandy. In Yemen, where public sale of alcoholic beverages was prohibited, you could not just go out to a store and buy alcoholic drinks. Therefore I kept my supply handy for social occasions such as when I invited guests to my apartment.

Before I went to the living room where the driver and Fred were waiting, I asked myself, could I out-drink Fred? I figured that if I could, he would probably sleep like a log, as they say, and I would not worry about him until it was time to pick him up for his doctor's appointment. I made sure I drank slowly, while I served my guest promptly whenever he requested more.

By the time we called it quits, I assumed Fred was ready to turn in to sleep and was in no position to get into any such problem as the caller may have alluded to. The driver, who had not touched any alcohol, helped us with the employee's luggage when we took him to his apartment. Then the driver and I sat there for a few minutes until Fred was finally fast asleep.

The following morning I called the physician before the driver picked up Fred for the ride to the embassy. I shared with the physician some of that conversation I had had with the long distance caller from the US. When I was at my office, I paced restlessly. My phone rang, and the doctor filled me in about his talk with Fred and subsequent decision. I waited for Fred, who I expected to come straight to the office from his doctor's appointment.

When he arrived he looked a bit bedraggled from a night of heavy drinking, but otherwise rather buoyant and relieved. "What's the verdict?" I asked. "I am going home!" he announced jubilantly. The secretary was on the phone immediately to arrange for his flight back to the United States the following day. Needless to say, I was greatly relieved that everything had turned out as well as could be for both of us. While it would have been nice to have an extra hand in the office, I was not too keen in having one who might turn out to be a burden at a time when I was trying to nurse the project back to health.

I did give serious thought afterwards as to whether I had done the right thing in being overly generous in sharing my

Fundador with him. In retrospect, I concluded that it was probably a reckless thing to do on my part. He could have been taking medicine that might have interacted adversely with the alcoholic drink, even if he disclaimed being on such medication when I asked him. With hindsight, I can say that I would not do that again. That time, I am thankful we were both lucky.

Tea For Two

I have not been much of an exponent of that dictum, "When in Rome do as the Romans do." On the other hand, I always had a standard advice when any of my former students, preparing to go overseas as Peace Corps volunteers or as teachers, came to bid me goodbye and ask for any last minute suggestions I might give them. I remember telling them to be "good listeners and observers." I reminded them, too, to be always on the lookout for their safety. But then travel can be replete with unforeseen challenges, and maybe that is part of the adventure.

While I was in the Philippines in 1953, I attended a wedding celebration in a village in the Mountain Province with other colleagues from the University of the Philippines. We were treated to some tribal dances and to a traditional wedding drink called *tapoy* (rice wine). We squatted on the ground in a large semicircle of probably twenty men, most of them in G-strings. The drinking began, and all was merriment. I felt jovial as well, until I looked down the row of men and saw what was coming. The drink was being ladled from an old and dented galvanized bucket that looked on the outside as if it had not been cleaned for ages. I watched apprehensively as the bucket came closer to me. When the common cup was finally given to me, I saw that it did not look any cleaner than the bucket. Inside the cup was some murky-looking liquid with rice in it, reminding me a bit of the leftover rice in a pot that had been soaked overnight for cleaning. Still, I lifted the cup in offering to the group. Then I brought the rim to my mouth without opening my lips, closed my eyes, held my breath, and pretended to drink! Fortunately, the cup was only half-full so that I was able to convincingly tilt the cup against my lips and hold it in that position briefly without opening my mouth. I wiped my mouth with the back of my hand as the others did. The person serving the drinks was probably too busy talking to the other men to notice what I did since I returned the cup into the bucket myself. I was out of that circle before the bucket came around for the second time.

While in Swaziland (1979-81), it was a bit of an embarrassment for me when I finally realized that I had been ignoring people who had been greeting me. The Swazis were so soft-spoken that I hardly heard the ever so gentle greeting, "*Saobona*," when they passed by while I was visiting the schools. Fortunately, I stayed in that country long enough to learn and understand this beautiful and gentle greeting, and I came to share a lot of pleasant memories with the Swazis.

But in North Yemen there was one gesture of welcome that I had to find some ways to avoid. I was told that it was customary to be served hot tea before special occasions such as when an important business deal is negotiated, someone's home is visited, or there is an extended visit to a government office. One time during a regular visit to a government office, I found myself waiting for the customary hot tea. I knew this tea would be refreshing and, indeed, I had been looking forward to it. Unfortunately, that day I happened to glance through the door into an adjoining room and, to my horror, I saw the custodian of the building "cleaning" the glasses in the business part of the toilet bowl! I am not going to generalize about that incident for it could have been just that lone custodian who had a particularly pragmatic way of dealing with the problem of water scarcity. But despite my efforts not to generalize, I decided I was done with the hot tea business whenever I visited that particular office.

Unfortunately, my job required regular visits to that office, and the tea kept coming! I did not touch my glass. With just my translator, the host and I, it was easily noticeable that I ignored my tea. I was later reprimanded good-naturedly by my translator, and told that I was in violation of protocol for not drinking my tea! I know, I admitted, but I had my special reason. I did not share the story with him, however. It was another week before my next visit, and that gave me some time to find a solution to that protocol dilemma. After all, the success of my mission depended partly upon a positive rapport with that wonderful host. Aha! I thought I had it! For our next trip, I told the translator about my plan. When the three glasses would be brought out on a tray and set on that small coffee table, I requested my translator to quickly finish his glass of tea. And then, when I was engaged in spirited discourse with my host, with distracting hand gestures, the translator was to switch his empty glass with mine. Fortunately, it worked quite smoothly. Thankfully, for the succeeding weeks, never did the nimble-fingered translator ever drink my host's glass of tea by mistake!

Planning with Filipino engineers how to meet a deadline for
a USAID project in North Yemen. The engineers completed
the project on time in fine style. 1985.

A visit to a village school outside Sanaa, North Yemen, 1984.

The author and Swazi World War II veterans
employed as security guards in our housing
compound in Manzini, Swaziland, 1979-1981.

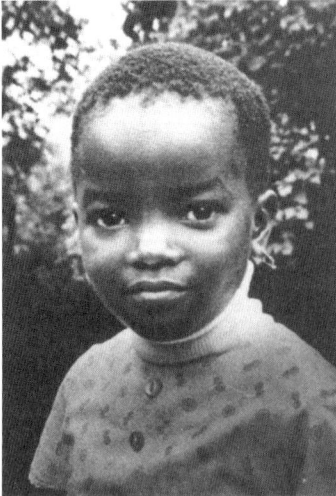

Swazi children from my neighborhood in Manzini,
Swaziland, who sometimes kept me company when I
worked in the garden. The enterprising ones sold me
oranges and other fruits in season. 1979-1981.

**Presenting a paper at the Comparative and
International Educational Society, Mexico City, 1997.**

Part IV
Travel

fiamente 2006

Jaywalking

Those familiar with the traffic in Manila in the 1950s can probably call to mind the congestion, the various colorful decorations on vehicles, and their state of near-decay judging from the asthmatic sound of the engines and the smoke from noisy tailpipes. There appeared to be wanton disregard of traffic rules, and the variety of religious invocations painted on public transportation was probably to insure against collisions and car "nappers." Pedestrian traffic was equally chaotic and congested, and walkers were just as daring as the bus or *jeepney* (jeeps converted for public transportation) drivers. In many places, there were designated crossings with painted markings on the street, a traffic policeman directing the traffic, and sometimes traffic lights. But jaywalking was a constant problem. People took their chances. They usually crossed in bunches, which probably gave them a sense of security.

While waiting to cross the busy Quezon Boulevard near Quiapo church when I was a college student, I sometimes took time to appraise the people around me and tried to guess their circumstances on the basis of how they were dressed. It was always easy to spot the *colegialas* (female students at parochial schools) with their uniforms; the ROTC cadets and the school with which they were associated from the patches on their shirts; peddlers of flowers, sweepstake tickets, wristwatches, religious cards, and *balot* (boiled, partially incubated duck's egg). Sometimes there would be well-dressed people who stood out, and who held their head high as if to distance themselves from the "common people" around them. One time, I saw a somewhat over-dressed woman, probably in her fifties, who had that air of superiority. From her double chin, she was obviously well-fed. She held her head up. I did not miss the tilt of the head because of her unusual hairdo. It was elaborately rolled and tapered to the top. I do not know what she thought about it, but to me it looked distinctly like a pile of moist cow dung. But then, style is a matter of individual taste.

When the traffic slowed down a minute, we all cautiously stepped into the opening and started walking to the other side. This time while crossing the wide boulevard, a booming announcement suddenly came from a public speaker. "It is against the law to jaywalk!" I was embarrassed and bewildered. I wondered where the voice was coming from. I hesitated, but since I was already halfway across, there was really no point in going back. "You with the uniform from the Holy Spirit, you with the ROTC uniform, you with the red umbrella, you with the funny hairdo," the loudspeaker went on. We accelerated our steps as the people at either side of the boulevard started laughing. But that was not all.

When we got across, there were three policemen at the other side waiting! They promptly cleared an area, rounded us up, and told us to follow them to a waiting van that was about a block away. I usually prided myself in getting out of tight spots, but I certainly was not prepared for this. As some of the bystanders started to crowd closer to look at us who got caught, the progress of the walk towards the van was slowed a bit. That gave me more time to think.

I slowed down more and more, and moved closer to the back of the pack towards the policeman herding us from the rear. I walked right next to him, and presented my story. I told him I was sorry, but I was rushing to the drugstore to get medicine for a sick relative. It was urgent, I added, that I get the medicine home right away. We were now about two-thirds of the way towards the police van. He was quiet. Then he said, "Break away from the group." He looked the other way, which I thought was a signal. I thanked him, walked more slowly until I separated from the group and merged with the onlookers. You would think that I would have moved away as quickly as I could. I did not. In fact I hung around with the bystanders to watch those arrested get loaded in the van. Call it sadism, but I just wanted to see the expression of that aristocratic woman with the funny hairdo as she was hustled into the police van.

Probinciano In
The Big City

Having just completed the first year as a university student in Manila, I looked forward to going back to my hometown of Laoag, Ilocos Norte for vacation. I eagerly anticipated many parties with other returning students, a visit to my old high school now that I had a new status, and a welcome change altogether from life in the big city. In the afternoon, a leisurely walk to the town plaza was a ritual. There, a handful of friends would congregate, talk, and pass the time. We would compare experiences as new students in Manila.

Unfortunately there was one who was a bit of a know-it-all. He was also a name-dropper, would brag about where the bargains were, and gossip about a socialite who was in the same class with him. And he had an irritating habit of occasionally interrupting and "correcting" a speaker, although his information sometimes turned out to be wrong. Other than that, Dadoy was a good enough fellow, and we took his shortcomings in stride, but allowed ourselves to laugh good-naturedly sometimes at his expense.

One time in Manila after my classes at the University of the Philippines were over for the day, I was on the way to my parents' apartment. Dadoy was with me for the first leg of my trip. He was also on his way to his boarding house. Since we had just completed our ROTC drill, we were still in uniform, complete with a tie. After reaching Quiapo, where we would take our respective connecting public transportation, he told me that there were some interesting movies that can be seen for a small fee in a vacant lot along Quezon Boulevard, not far from the Quiapo church. This aroused my curiosity, and I followed him. I was puzzled, however, that the location of the movies was in a vacant lot. We walked for two blocks to the location where there were four small temporary sheds made of galvanized iron sheets. A shed was about ten by fifteen feet, had one little door, and no windows. Each had a small projector, and there was an announcer who informed the curious about the selections, the cost, and starting time. A show lasted about twenty minutes, and they charged twenty-five centavos per person. There were two live strip-tease sheds, the third was a film on "revelations from a nudist camp," and the fourth was, we thought, the most daring: a frontal view of a woman giving birth! That was our choice.

I figured I had enough for a ticket with a little leftover for my fare from Quiapo to Lealtad. I counted my twenty-five centavos and handed it to the announcer. Dadoy and I walked in. There were at least fifteen people standing inside that hot shed, staring at a little screen close to the ceiling. I stood there in the

First aid by Dadoy

midst of the sweaty spectators, and tried to focus on the tiny screen as my eyes adjusted to the dark interior. Meanwhile the horns of the jeeps passing by blared incessantly. After about ten minutes in that dungeon, I began to feel faint, lost consciousness, and collapsed. When I came to, I was outside the shed on the ground with Dadoy fanning me. The fact that we were packed like sardines probably kept me from falling hard. After a while, I got up and dusted myself off. I later walked over to the jeep terminal for Lealtad and went home.

Dadoy never forgot that incident, which he claimed was due to my weak stomach, and that I could not stand to see a woman giving birth! Of course I always countered that it was just a poorly ventilated shed that was hot and crowded. To my chagrin and embarrassment, Dadoy would relate that event when we were swapping stories in Laoag with the other boys about our adventures as *probincianos* in the big city.

At one of these gatherings at the Laoag Plaza, he revealed another of his "finds" in Manila. He asked if we were familiar with a particular movie house towards the north end of Avenida Rizal. We did not usually venture in that direction, but we were familiar with some aspects of that location since the bus from Ilocos Norte passed through that part of Avenida Rizal. Dadoy said that he went there usually to see a movie, which was quite cheap. But more enticing than the movie was that sometimes a young lady, he claimed, came to sit next to him for some "intimate pleasures." You did not have to pay, he said, but a tip was always appreciated. Without being specific, he said that was the best part of going to that movie house. He obviously enjoyed watching us speculate on the hinted subtleties of his story with imagined specifics. Dadoy enjoyed our attention. He was in his glory when he thought he could trump all our stories.

Innocently, I made the observation that that area abounded with *bakla* (homosexuals) and cross-dressers. The whole group was quiet for a while, but only briefly. Finally realizing what Dadoy had probably gotten into, they exploded with laughter. Obviously he had not considered the reputation of that neighborhood when he began bragging about this experience in the big city. Only as everyone laughed did he probably wonder who those "young ladies" were who sat next to him for his afternoon delights. He was dumbstruck, and never again did he talk about his adventures in the big city.

Village Of
Al-Maghris

From the ancient town of Zabid, five of us (the driver, a school headmaster, a representative from the Ministry of Education, a translator, and I) set out in a four-wheel-drive vehicle in the general direction of the Red Sea towards the village of Al-Maghris. The street we followed out of town soon deteriorated into a rugged road of sand and stones. The tire tracks of previous vehicles were hardly noticeable as thick clouds of dust blew across our path.

Farther from Zabid, the surrounding began to look more like a desert. It was an expanse of sandy landscape broken now and then by a solitary date palm that stood like a sentinel over the land. Once in a while a Bedouin camp would appear. They were marked by a fence of sticks and small branches that served as an enclosure for a few animals that included camels, goats, sheep, and donkeys. Sometimes it appeared that the human shelter in these nomadic camps was not much more than a lean-to of branches with a piece of cloth or skin draped on one side as protection from the wind or the rays of the sun. Where there were children, it was touching to see them interrupt their play to wave at us. I readied my camera because I decided these camp settings would make a good photo. At that point, however, I was advised by my Yemeni companions not to take pictures. They were not sure, they cautioned, how the Bedouins would react. When my companions added that they sometimes had guns, I took note and promptly put my camera away.

Having heard about Bedouins mostly from popularized accounts, I was curious what stereotypes the Yemenis had about them. "What is a Bedouin?" I asked. The essence of their response was, "They are people who do not like to live in towns. They move from one place to another. We respect them. They are good people." Consulting another source, the Arabist Raphael Patai, gives the following description from his book *The Arab Mind*:

> What kind of person is this Bedouin to whom relationship is claimed by high and low alike in settled Arab society? We may begin by stating that he is son and master of the desert, whose way of life has changed very little from the time he domesticated the camel in the eleventh or twelfth century B.C. until the penetration of his ancestral habitat by modern technology in search for oil. For three thousand years, the desert was his impregnable stronghold: here the Bedouin could preserve undisturbed the way of life he had developed in close symbiosis with his camel, the "ship of the desert." In the desert he was able to guard his sacred traditions, the purity of his language and his blood, and develop a unique social and cultural adaptation to one of the harshest environments known to man on earth. (Patai, p. 76)

Although the distance from Zabid to Al-Maghris was about twelve kilometers, it took us nearly an hour to travel. As we came closer to our destination, the green of the vegetation became more noticeable, and the village of Al-Maghris finally came into view. My first impression was that of a cluster of flat-roofed, one-story houses, probably made of mud brick, surrounded by high mud walls. The top of the trees and date palms swayed in the breeze, a refreshing sight after driving through a sandy and barren landscape.

Surrounding the village were scattered patches of cultivated land that looked dry and cracked, at least from my perspective as one familiar with the lush and green farm fields of Ilocos Norte in the Philippines, and those of Michigan. The plants looked sparse and the leaves were coated with dust. Water supply was apparently quite limited. The rainy season was short. There were no large bodies of fresh surface water. The dry riverbeds were inundated periodically, but did not retain much of the water as it flowed into the Red Sea. The little water absorbed by the porous and sandy riverbed became part of the ground water, and that was the main source that sustained agriculture. The water was drawn from hand-dug wells with the aid of a pail hoisted manually or, for the more fortunate, it was siphoned with the use of a mechanized pump. The life-giving water flowed into narrow and shallow canals that radiated like arteries to different sections of the fields. There were little depressions around the stem of each cultivated plant to help retain the precious water.

Al-Maghris had three clusters of houses with approximately a few hundred inhabitants who were mostly farmers. It was estimated that over one hundred of the young men were currently working abroad. Farming in the village consisted mainly of growing cotton, watermelon, millet, jasmine, sesame, tomato, onion, pepper, and okra. Dates were also an important part of the economy. I was told that most of what the farmers produced was consumed in the village, and only a small portion was sold at the public market. The herding of sheep, goats, and cattle supplemented the economy of the village, and these were used mostly as source of meat for local consumption. Remittances from the young men who worked abroad provided an important source of currency. The headmaster who accompanied us said there were three generators in the village bought by some of the workers who returned from abroad. "Now most of the households have TV, including video."

The village had one school, grades one through six, with two hundred fifty students (boys and girls). Two Sudanese teachers managed the school. Classes were held mostly outdoors in the courtyard of the school because of lack of classroom space.

After our school visit we drove closer to one of the clusters of houses, and we parked the vehicle in front of a large gate. A tall man, probably in his sixties, came out to greet us. He shook our hands through the car window. The headmaster who was with us introduced him as the vice chief of the village. After the headmaster explained who we were, the vice chief seemed satisfied and glad. He motioned the vehicle to be driven through the gate.

We drove into a large enclosure where there were two Toyota pickup trucks and a Suzuki motorcycle. I assumed these were purchased with remittances from Yemeni members of the family working abroad. The enclosed parking area was connected to another walled section by a narrow gate with a metal door about three feet wide. We followed the vice chief through the door and emerged into a corral. There were five cows, three sheep, and a donkey. I did not ask if they had other animals in the field. Along the inner wall of the corral there were three small gates with small metal doors. Each of these three doors opened into a separate enclosed courtyard with two small mud-and-stick buildings allocated for each nuclear family. One building, I was told, was for sleeping. The other was for eating. The basic arrangement was such that, while the members of the extended family resided within the large enclosure surrounded by high mud walls about ten feet high, it was subdivided into sections which provided some privacy for each nuclear family, and a separate space for the animals and for the vehicles.

The vice chief guided us through one of the small gates in the inner wall into his courtyard with its own building for living space and a small one for eating. In the courtyard were a water faucet, some potted ornamental plants, and some laundry drying in the sun. I asked who all the kids and young men were who followed us into the vice chief's courtyard. The vice chief laughed after my question was translated, and then he pointed proudly to himself. As it turned out, he and his wife had four married sons and a daughter. The small ones were his grandchildren.

We entered his living quarters. It was a one-room building of mud brick with dirt floor. I estimated the size of the room to be about twenty-four by fifteen feet. Lined end to end along three walls were long chairs shaped like sofa beds about four feet high. In front of these were another row of sofa beds but only about two feet high. There were ten of these tall and short ones combined, and each one was covered with brightly colored blankets and some little cushions.

The walls were whitewashed. About ten feet from the floor was a ledge that protruded about six inches from each of three walls. On these ledges were plates, aluminum pots, and basins. There were a few framed pictures from, I assumed, Islamic history. A prayer mat was hung on the wall.

Each of us was assigned a sofa bed where we reclined or squatted. Not long after we got ourselves settled, two boys brought in soft drinks and some hot sweet tea. As it was almost noontime, I decided to stretch my legs. I walked to the section where I had seen animals earlier. Two of the young men had a sheep suspended from the rafter, expertly cut to pieces and cleaned. I was informed it was going to be prepared for our lunch. The headmaster explained that hospitality, even to strangers, was a well-known trait of the Arabs. The slaughter of a sheep indicated an honored guest was being hosted, and the longer the visitors stayed, even as long as three days, the better the status of the host in the eyes of his neighbors.

The vice chief also had a second roofed structure in his yard that looked more like a poorly constructed shed. That is where we had our lunch. It was a small space, somewhat tight for the six men. We squatted on the dirt floor and formed a circle around the rice and lamb served on a huge platter set on oilcloth over the dirt floor. A dented aluminum cup with soup in it was passed around and refilled as needed. I had my turn at the cup, too. I sat next to the vice chief. He sort of eyed me as I scooped some rice with my hand, formed it into a ball and put into my mouth. He laughed and shook his head. He showed me how it should be done. He reached for the rice, probably three times the amount I got for myself with one scoop. He balled this expertly and put that into his mouth. The rest chuckled at the demonstration. I got the message, and dug in like everybody else. The vice chief looked pleased.

Before I end my recollection of that memorable trip to Al-Maghris, I should mention a quiet conversation I had with the vice chief as we prepared to return to Hodeida. With Ibrahim, who was his nephew and my translator, the vice chief took us aside away from the other men. He asked if I had my wife with me in Sanaa. When I informed him that I did not, he expressed shock that I was without a woman. With that as introduction, the vice chief suggested I should stay as his guest at least for the weekend in the company of one of the young women from the village. I checked with Ibrahim if I heard the translation right. Ibrahim, with a twinkle in his eye, assured me that I heard him right. Arabian nights? I thanked the vice chief for his kindness. I informed him I had a meeting scheduled in Hodeida the following morning, and, therefore, could not possibly stay for the weekend. He said he understood and assured me that I was always welcome to visit his village again.

Roman Holiday

The first time I was in Rome was when I attended a conference to present a paper and to promote Eastern Michigan University's overseas program for teachers. I did not spend time as a tourist then, so I vowed that at my next visit I would make an effort to see some of the attractions of that historic city. My opportunity came in the form of a policy governing the travel of personnel for USAID-funded projects. This allowed the traveler an overnight stop if the duration of the journey from an overseas assignment to home base or vice versa took more than fourteen hours. Fortunately, my assignments with EMU as subcontractor for USAID projects overseas involved destinations like Swaziland and North Yemen that required more than fourteen hours of travel. My work also required relatively frequent returns to the United States for conferences either in Washington DC or at Eastern Michigan University.

On one of my trips from North Yemen to the United States,

I requested my secretary to arrange my travel to include a three-day stop in Rome. She asked if I had any preference for a hotel. When I travel as a tourist, I usually prefer to spend a more leisurely time in one or two locations instead of dashing hurriedly from one place to another just to be able to say that I have been there. Therefore, I suggested to the secretary that I would prefer a hotel close to either the Vatican or the Spanish Steps, the two places I wanted to see during my three-day stopover. At the Vatican, I was mainly interested in looking at how the restoration of Michelangelo's painting of the ceiling of the Sistine Chapel was coming along. As to the Spanish Steps, I was just curious to see it, since I often read about it. As I expected, the secretary told me it was easier to get a hotel room close to the Spanish Steps than around the Vatican. I said that was good enough, as long as the hotel was not a fleabag and it was within walking distance to the Spanish Steps.

I arrived at my hotel early in the afternoon. It was in a clean and quiet neighborhood. The surrounding buildings were old but they looked nicely maintained. The little stores were conservatively and tastefully decorated. The people around were well dressed and vehicular traffic was relatively sparse. All in all, it was a neat and pleasant setting. I entered my hotel, registered, and went to my room. I had a quick shower and a short nap. Somehow the excitement of preparing for a major trip usually keeps me awake the night before, and if I have to get up early to go to the airport it becomes even more tiring. Thus, it was good to feel refreshed and rested before venturing out for a walk around the block where my hotel was located. It was getting close to five o'clock in the afternoon by the time I was ready to leave.

For my first afternoon, I planned a leisurely walk around to look into the small shops, check the fruit stand at the corner, and enjoy a cup of coffee in front of the shop with tiny tables on the sidewalk. What a restful change, I thought, to be physically and psychologically removed, even for a short time, from the drudgery of going to the office every day in Yemen. I did not forget, however, that putting up with the humdrum of office work in Yemen and all that it entailed made such pleasure trips possible. On balance, I thought it was a good assignment, considering all the fringe benefits. It was with these thoughts finally tucked away in my mind that I stepped out of the hotel into a nice, mild, and sunny afternoon.

I stood briefly in front of the hotel to check my bearings and to decide which direction I should take. I was just about ten yards from the hotel when a middle-aged man, wearing a conservatively cut suit and a clean white shirt with a tie, approached me in a polite and friendly way. Somewhat hesitatingly, he asked if I spoke English, and would I be interested in a female companion while I was in Rome? To the man, I was obviously a tourist, and probably mistaken for a Japanese businessman. Notwithstanding how well-dressed he was, and how refined his manners, a word flashed through my mind: "Pimp!"

I must admit, however, that my immediate reaction was not a negative one. I felt somewhat flattered initially by the proposition since it meant, among other things, that I probably looked prosperous enough to be so approached and that I looked physically able to enjoy the delights of a Roman holiday! "On the other hand," as Topol used to say in *Fiddler on the Roof* when he was faced with a dilemma, maybe I looked gullible enough to be so propositioned. In any case, I politely thanked him while we walked, and told him I had other things I planned to do while in Rome. But he was persistent as he described the choices in term of the age of the women, command of English, duration, what they could do, and other items on the menu. Other people strolling on the sidewalk could have easily thought the two well-dressed men were discussing quietly some corporate merger of international conglomerates rather than the international merger of more modest proportions that we were actually discussing. After walking with me for about twenty minutes, he politely thanked me and left, probably to station himself again in front of the hotel in search of other potential customers.

Finally by myself, I started window-shopping. A small shop of handsomely tailored sport coats caught my eye. I stopped in front of the display window, assessed the merchandise, and pondered whether I should go in. Just then I noticed a young lady was standing next to me. She greeted me and we exchanged pleasantries. Then she asked what hotel I was staying in, and if I would like to give her my room number. I turned to look at her. I guessed she could have been in her twenties. She was pretty, I thought, and neatly dressed rather in the manner of a college student, and with hardly any makeup. She was soft-spoken and appeared refined. She did not look at all like the stereotype of a hooker. Not wanting to be rude, I commented that she was very attractive and refined, but I had a business meeting scheduled for the night. I thought she was probably the pimp's second line of persuasion. If so, he was certainly orchestrating a smooth-running operation. Before the woman left, she wondered if the following day would be a better time. I said I was not sure because if the business meeting that evening was not successful, my business partners and I would have to meet again before I returned home.

After the young woman left me, I resumed my walk towards the coffee shop. It had such tiny tables, I thought, they could not possibly be shared by two people. I picked out a chair after the waiter standing outside pointed to one of the empty tables. After figuring out the various choices, I ordered a cup of coffee and relaxed, just enjoying watching the people. Another woman came to my table and asked if she could share the table with me. I nodded. She motioned to the waiter to put an extra chair across from me. She looked like she could have been a secretary and was stopping for coffee on her way home. She started to converse with me. It was not long before I concluded she wanted more than a cup of coffee. After I gave her the same excuse as the previous lady, she finally left.

I drank my coffee, but I was beginning to feel a bit irritated with the intrusions. I wondered how I could deal with it so that I could enjoy the rest of my stay. I had dinner later somewhere in the neighborhood. Back at the hotel that evening, I asked the concierge of the hotel where I could pick up a taxi or a bus for the Vatican the following morning. I turned in for the night.

The painting on the ceiling of the Sistine Chapel, one of the great works of Michelangelo, was undergoing cleaning and restoration. Through a complicated process of x-ray and chemical analysis, experts claimed to have been able to identify the original paint applied by Michelangelo, and thus were

Would you give me your hotel room number?

able to separate layers of grime and retouching by later artists. The time of my visit was very interesting since only half of the ceiling was restored and one could clearly see the contrast between the two sections. The older section had muted tones. The part that was already cleaned was bright and the colors were bold and brilliant but, in my opinion, a bit gaudy.

It was at the Sistine Chapel that I hit on a plan to deal with the pimp and his seductive companions. I knew they would confront me again when I got back to the neighborhood. I took a shower and rested briefly before venturing out again for an afternoon walk.

Sure enough, when I left the hotel, there was the pimp again, all set to entice me once more with the pleasures of a Roman holiday. This time I was ready for him. Assuming a benign and forgiving expression, I made the sign of the cross over him. And in a solemn voice, I uttered some fake Latin like "chocolate colorum, ominus pobiscum." I moved my right hand in an act of blessing him. I continued: "I am a priest, my son. I pray for God's forgiveness and for your protection from eternal damnation." I repeated my pretend Latin to finalize my blessing, "Chocolate colorum, ominus pobiscum." I wish you could have seen how his eyes got wider. "*Excusi, excusi*, Father. You *looke normale*." Almost in disbelief, he repeated, "You *looke normale*." With a sweaty and horrified look, he bowed slightly and beat a hasty retreat.

I resumed my walk, the same route I took the day before. What a peaceful afternoon after that. Although I was not impervious, by any means, to the tempting possibilities offered by attractive women, I rationalized that the recklessness of youth was a luxury I could no longer afford now that I was a family man. The health and well-being of those close to me, as well as those of other people with whom I came in contact had become a more important consideration.

"Chocolate colorum, ominus pobiscum."

Missing A
Passport In Cairo

The parking lot of the Cairo International Airport in Egypt looked deserted at three-thirty that morning, December 26, 1984, except for two elderly men warming themselves by a flickering fire on that cold winter day. The taxi that had brought me now sped away, its red backlights gradually obscured by the early morning fog. I had just discovered that my passport case, which I had placed in my winter jacket, was missing.

Realization of the magnitude and complexity of my predicament hit me like a flash. I could not speak Arabic and the two men warming themselves in the parking lot were obviously laborers and would not have been able to respond to me in English. In my missing passport case were my travel papers: US passport, visa for re-entry to North Yemen, airline ticket to the United States and return, and about a thousand dollars in cash. To make matters worse, my flight to the United States was scheduled to depart at six o'clock that morning in exactly

Did I drop it in the taxi?

two and a half hours. How did I ever find myself in such a predicament? And I thought I was an experienced international traveler?

When I traveled, I tended to wear my long-sleeved safari shirt because of its large, buttoned pockets. The pockets were convenient for separating my passport, tickets, traveler's checks, etc., and these items were safe and accessible. What had gone awry this time was that I had started from Yemen, with its mild winter, had an overnight stop in Cairo, and was enroute to Michigan's wintery weather. I had started with my safari shirt from Yemen, but then decided to change into my heavier winter jacket at the

Sheraton Hotel in Cairo before leaving for the airport at three o'clock that morning. I noticed then that the pockets of my winter jacket were not closable, but I had rationalized that it was just a thirty-minute drive from the hotel to the airport, and surely not enough time for anything to go wrong.

Why, you may ask, had I put all the important items in one container? Another mistake, but I thought then that I needed to consolidate them because of the change into this jacket that did not have very many pockets. Why carry so much cash, instead of traveler's checks? Keeping a large amount of cash in the office safe in Yemen was a precautionary measure for USAID-funded projects. The Yemeni banks were not always reliable for changing Yemeni *reals* to US dollars. So, we were advised by the USAID office in Yemen to keep some dollars in cash for emergencies like immediate trips back to the US or quick getaways from Yemen to another country. My decision to return to Michigan for the Christmas holiday had been an impulsive one. As I stood there dumbfounded, in the wee hours of a chilly Cairo morning, these were the thoughts that flashed through my mind.

I had two and a half hours remaining before departure time, and no passport, air ticket, or money. I knew I was in big, big trouble! I felt a weakening of my knees, a sensation I had never felt before. My mouth was dry, and my heart seemed to be pounding more rapidly than usual. At the same time, I reminded myself that I could not yield to panic, or I would never solve my problem. Given the limited time I had, I knew I needed to (a) get a hold of myself, and (b) be economical in my choice of possible solutions, for I did not have much time for trial and error.

I formed a system in my mind, and followed it. I established a set of assumptions: (a) my passport case popped out of my pocket when I sat down in the taxi, (b) taxi drivers usually had areas assigned to them and, therefore, my taxi probably went back to the Sheraton, and (c) the driver was not aware of my passport in the back seat. Since it was so early in the morning, I also entertained the hope that the driver had not yet picked up another fare who could have found the passport case with money in it.

Based on these assumptions, I determined a quick plan of action. The first thing to do was to get back to the Sheraton as soon as possible. But there were no taxis, no private cars, and the building closest to me looked dark. The highway was too far from where I was, and it was not a good place to hitch a ride, not to mention I was unable to communicate in Arabic.

After about ten minutes, a man emerged from one of the buildings. He looked to be a white-collar employee. I approached him, and greeted him hoping desperately that he would return my greetings in English. To my great relief, he did. I told him what my problem was, and that I needed to go back to the Sheraton hotel quickly. He said there was not much traffic coming to where we were since there were only a few flights that early in the morning. He offered to stay with me, and help me if he could, however.

In another five minutes, an empty taxi drove by. My new companion flagged him down, and he went over to talk to the driver. The driver told him he could not go to the Sheraton because that was not his area. I was devastated, but I was consoled by the thought that one of my assumptions was correct:

taxi drivers were assigned areas of operation. My companion pleaded with the taxi driver, and the driver decided to take me to the Sheraton. On the way to the hotel, I continued to explore in my mind alternative solutions. If I could not find my passport case, I still had my wallet with enough money to pay the driver, and I had my credit card to stay at the Sheraton. It would be a better place, I thought, from which to call the US Embassy to report my missing passport, etc., and to call my office in Yemen to obtain for me another re-entry visa to Yemen. These alternatives were necessary, I thought, just in case the driver or a passenger found the passport case with the one thousand dollars in cash and decided to keep it.

We finally reached the Sheraton after a thirty-minute drive from the airport. The driver said he would wait for me so he could drive me to wherever I needed to go. It was already four-fifteen in the morning, less than two hours from my scheduled departure time. I went straight to the lobby which was almost empty except for a handful of employees sitting around. They recognized me and expressed surprise since they had just loaded my luggage into the taxi about an hour ago. I told them I left a "piece of luggage" in the taxi, and would they know the taxi driver and where he was? The young man who loaded my luggage said that he knew the driver and that the taxis were parked beside the hotel. Somebody ordered one of the boys to fetch the driver.

I paced back and forth in the lobby. I was obviously agitated, and one of the employees gestured for me to take it easy. The boy came back to report that the taxi driver was no longer at his parking station. The employees started discussing where else he could be. One possibility was that he could have gone to a favorite coffee shop for taxi drivers nearby, or he could have gone home. It was already close to four-thirty. The employees decided to get one of the taxis still in the hotel parking lot to check the coffee shop and, if the driver was not there, to drive straight to his house.

Now it was nearly five o'clock. I decided to go outside for I felt the air inside the lobby was almost suffocating. Soon a set of headlights appeared in the driveway, and then another. There were two taxis, and out jumped the drivers. One of them was waving my passport case. I hugged the driver. I went into the hotel lobby, changed some dollars into Egyptian money, and distributed tips all around. I do not remember how much. All the employees were jubilant as I got into the taxi that drove me back to the airport. It was the same taxi that took me to the Sheraton and had waited for me all that time.

It was almost six o'clock when we arrived back at the airport. I tipped the driver handsomely as I kept saying, "*Shokran. Shokran.*" (Thank you.) It was the only Arabic I remembered then. I rushed to the departure gate, but when I got there it was dark. I wondered if I was in the wrong building, or did I misunderstand the schedule? It was a sinking feeling, I can tell you that! Just then two security guards came to check who I was. They informed me the passengers had left. After explaining that I was a passenger, they spoke to someone through their intercom system. They loaded my luggage in their van and drove me to the plane which was warming up for takeoff. I breathlessly boarded the plane, sank into my seat, and resumed my flight to Michigan.

Mozambique

I wanted to visit Mozambique before I completed my assignment in Swaziland in 1981. The idea of a trip was prompted by a number of considerations: (1) It had been under Portuguese rule since 1498, and designated as an overseas province in 1952. I was curious to see what influence of Portugal may have remained, at least in the style of buildings in its capital, Maputo. (2) The country had gone through one of the most brutal wars in southern Africa, and a Soviet-backed anti-colonial movement took power in 1974. Most of the approximately 180,000 whites had left the country. I had actually seen the influx of refugees, both whites and blacks, into Swaziland. What kind of a country had the refugees left behind? Mozambique was reported to have a population of over twelve million in 1980, one of the poorest countries in the world with a per capita gross product estimated at eighty US dollars. It had an illiteracy rate of 93 percent. (3) Maputo as a seaport promised fresh seafood, which I could enjoy there, and perhaps even bring some back to land-locked Swaziland where it was hard to get.

The prospect of making that trip, however, was not very bright. Guerrillas were still active in the countryside. I understood the position of the US embassy in issuing a travel advisory in 1981 after a couple of western journalists were reported missing in Mozambique.

Not willing to give up my plan to visit Mozambique, I kept track of the position of the US embassy. After about two weeks, I heard that the travel ban was lifted. A call to the embassy confirmed that, and I was advised to inform them of my plans such as where I would stay, how I was going to travel, and for how long. When I finally applied for a visa, however, I found out the Mozambique mission was ambivalent about issuing travel permits. After another week of no progress in obtaining the necessary travel documents, I was about to give up the whole idea.

I mentioned my predicament to a Portuguese friend who was a refugee in Swaziland. He was a businessman and had maintained his contacts with the people at the Mozambique mission. He informed me he could probably get a visa for me, but he wondered about my safety. He called my attention to the missing journalists, that the rebels were active in the rural areas, and that there were long stretches of uninhabited land along the highway from the border of Swaziland to Maputo.

A Swazi friend told me about a young man from Mozambique who was attending high school in Swaziland and who went home to Maputo on weekends for vacation. Since I was planning to drive my car by myself, my Swazi friend thought the young man would appreciate the ride, be a useful guide, and also make the trip safer for me. It looked like things were finally shaping up: a cautious green light from the US embassy, a visa from the Mozambique mission, and a guide. I should also mention that a few weeks earlier, I had met a couple of Filipinos working for the UN and stationed in Maputo. They happened to be visiting the Filipino doctors at the Nazarene Hospital in Manzini. They gave me their address with an open invitation to stay with them should I visit Mozambique. I notified them about my plans to be sure that the address had not changed and that they were not away for vacation.

I left with my guide on a Friday around mid-morning and got to Maputo in the evening. A drive around the town the following day after my arrival in Maputo showed some white-washed houses with red tile roofs, a touch of Portugal indeed. I assumed the previous owners probably no longer occupied those houses. Show windows of the stores were empty, and there were hardly any people around. When I finally saw a small cluster of people in what looked like a plaza, I slowed down to see what the attraction or activity was. They were native Africans who were waiting for their turn to buy ice cream from a vendor.

As far as seafood was concerned, my Filipino hosts told me that the Russians had effectively depleted the harvest from the sea. They came with their huge fishing vessels complete with processing equipment, and presumably sold their catch else-where. My hosts suggested we could go to the fishing village to wait for the local fishermen in small dugouts who brought in whatever catch they had. The fishermen would sell their catch right there on the seashore. We sat for a while under the shade of a tree and waited as four dugouts approached the shore. I bought crabs that my hosts boiled for me so I could take them back to Swaziland.

Saturday evening we went to a restaurant. My hosts warned me that customers could not count on what was available, but we should try anyway. Fortunately they had langoustines— large shrimps—that evening. For a huge platter of it, enough for three adults and two children, washed down with their local beer, I paid the equivalence of two dollars.

My hosts changed some dollars for me since the rate at a government bank was quite low, as expected. Purchases at restaurants or in the public market were transacted privately with more favorable rates for the dollar. Exchange of currency with a government agency was unavoidable, however, when I wanted to buy gasoline for my trip back. I was required to go to a government office to purchase gasoline coupons based on the government exchange rate, and then use the coupons at a gasoline station.

My hosts helped me load the car for the trip back. The woodcarvings I had bought at the public market were packed carefully, and the boiled crabs were kept cold in the refrigerator until the last minute. But realizing that I was making the trip back by myself, I was a bit apprehensive. It was mid-morning by the time I started driving.

I was just at the outskirt of Maputo when I was stopped at what looked like a military checkpoint. A man in uniform approached the car on the driver's side. He said something in a dialect that I did not understand. I responded in English. He gestured, pointing to a glum-looking man in a camouflaged uniform standing about five yards away from my car. He had a heavy bandoleer with hand grenades attached to it, and he was holding what looked like an automatic rifle. I still did not understand what the guard wanted me to do. He pointed to the other man again, and then pointed in the direction I was going. Although I was not sure, I chanced on the interpretation that I was being asked to give the heavily armed man a ride. Realizing that I probably did not have any choice, I nodded.

The guard gestured to the other man to come over. The armed man approached the car, opened the passenger door, got in, and shut the door. I looked at him with a faint smile. He just looked at me without any expression whatsoever. I tried to look calm and waved to the guard as I drove away.

If I have ever found myself in a situation where I was scared and felt utterly helpless, that would have been it. I could not engage my passenger in small talk, I did not know what he was up to, and he was heavily armed. The travel advisory, news about missing journalists, and reports about atrocities and roving guerillas came rushing back. I tried to whistle to ease the atmosphere in the car, but no sound would come out. My mouth was dry, and it was difficult to swallow.

It was probably another three hours to the border of Mozambique and Swaziland. I drove for miles without much vehicular traffic, and the villages were so far apart from each other. It was driving through these long stretches of desolation that I started hatching how I could survive in case my passenger had plans of his own about me. I decided that if he gestured for me to stop the car and for me to get out in a belligerent way, I would grab his gun as quickly as possible and

My silent hitchhiker.

with all the strength I could muster. I realized I did not know how to operate his rifle, but I intended to use it as a club, and then I would drag his body towards the shrubs along the road. I also figured I could reach Swaziland before anyone would discover his body.

That my mind had descended to that level made me feel degraded and guilty. I hoped fervently that such a horrible scenario would never come to pass. I realized, too, that my imagined pre-emptive action of clubbing the man before he got to me, was based on nothing more than hurriedly formulated assumptions.

After another thirty minutes or so, we came upon a village. The sight of huts and people in the vicinity made me feel safer. My silent companion gestured for me to slow down and stop. When I finally came to a full stop within the village, he turned towards me. He extended his hand to shake my hand, then he got out of the car. I felt exhausted but greatly relieved. I eased the car forward. I looked back through my rearview mirror.

I saw a couple of kids run towards him and some adults followed, I assumed, to welcome him home.

Welcome home, soldier. 1981.

Good-Hearted Strangers

I t would be misleading if the book left the impression that all I can remember from my travels and that of my family were the tight spots and occasional unsavory characters encountered along the way. Just as prominent in my memory and even more pleasant to remember are the good-hearted strangers we met. From them were unsolicited acts of thoughtfulness that underscored how kind people can be toward one another. The following are assorted experiences from different times and settings.

I recalled in my other book, *At the Table with the Family*, how total strangers offered shelter and even food to my father and brother as they made their long and dangerous journey from Manila to Laoag, immediately after the invasion of the Philippines by Japan. I mentioned, too, the hospitality of the people of Solsona in the province of Ilocos Norte who welcomed evacuees like my family into their midst and shared what scarce commodities they had even as we all economized in order to survive the war years. There were other stories of kindness, and the following are just a few of them.

How well I remember the first day the family moved into the house where we were to stay for the academic year while I was an exchange professor in England. There was a knock at the door. When I opened it, there was a well-dressed woman holding a tray with a teapot, some cookies, and a bouquet of flowers. With a smile she introduced herself as our next-door neighbor. She expressed concern that since we had just moved in, it was possible, she thought, that our gas was not yet connected. So there she was, a complete stranger to us, who wanted to be sure we did not miss our afternoon tea! And that was not the end of her warm and thoughtful gestures. For the entire year that we lived in that house, our good neighbor occasionally knocked at our door with some fresh-cut flowers from her beautiful garden.

Our year in England provided wonderful opportunities to visit, in our Volkswagen camper, different regions of Europe each time we had a long vacation between school terms. One such trip was in April, 1968, when we drove through France on our way to northern Italy. While in Paris, the family decided to visit the Louvre. We finished our tour of the museum around five o'clock in the afternoon. We decided to have dinner in the city before going back to our campsite, and we stopped at a small restaurant. It was empty except for a woman and a man sitting at one of the tables. It was nice to be indoors since it was rather cold outside. Before we could sit down, the woman called to our attention that they were not open yet. I suggested that we could wait until they open, if that was possible, since it was cold outside. "No!" she said gruffly. We left that inhospitable place, took a taxi, and found a more accommodating restaurant on the way to our campsite.

I could not help but note the contrast between our experience with the restaurant in Paris and the one we had in Italy at a fishing village near Vericchio. It was early afternoon when we arrived at a small restaurant. The owner greeted us warmly. When we informed him that we would like to have dinner, he politely told us that it was "too early." After a moment of silence, he noticed Cristina and Cynthia. He exclaimed, "Ah, *bambinas*! For you, I open." The man suggested he could take our orders, we could go for a short walk along the shore, and our dinner would be ready when we came back. What a heart-warming experience I thought. So much for April in Paris!

On our second trip, we decided to visit northern Europe via Holland to see the land of Judy's ancestors on her father's side, to Germany to have the Volkswagen bus fitted with camping equipment, and later on to Denmark mainly to visit Hans Christian Andersen's house.

While in northern Holland, we parked at a small campsite run by a family in Delden. We were there when the United States landed the first man on the moon. It was late at night, but many of the campers from different countries were still in the camp restaurant waiting for that historic event. The owner played the guitar and sang some popular World War II songs. Coffee and cookies were on the house while we eagerly awaited the moon landing. As pictures unfolded on a small television screen in the restaurant, how touching and uplifting it was that we witnessed that historic achievement of man without any thought of nationality. We all cheered warmly and proudly without any flag-waving.

Later at the campsite, I happened to mention to the camp owner that the ancestor's of Judy's dad were from Holland. "They are from Friesland," he said when I mentioned the family name "Elzinga." He seemed pleased and excited about Judy's ties to Holland, however remote they might be. He said that a group of country folks in their costumes were coming to the camp that afternoon to perform some traditional dances. Noticing that I had a movie camera, he suggested that I reserve some film for the occasion. He was obviously disappointed when I told him that I had just run out of film! He excused himself, and I did not see him again for another hour. He showed up later at our tent to announce that he found an extra film from one of the campers, and that I should use it only to film the folk dancers so that I could show it to my father-in-law when I returned to the United States. During the performance of the folk dancers he checked on me once in a while to be sure that I was filming. He also arranged to have one of the folk dancers select my wife as a partner when they started dancing with members of the audience.

On another occasion, since it was close to lunchtime when we finally crossed into Denmark, we decided to park and have our sandwiches inside the van in a tree-lined neighborhood of single-family houses. Just as Judy set up the little table in the van, a small car maneuvered into the parking space in front of us. A man got out of the car, turned briefly toward our direction, and went into one of the houses. I speculated at that time that he was probably a worker who had come home for lunch. After about half an hour, the man came out of the house, knocked at the window of our van, and handed me three bottles of soft drink that, from his gesture, were for Judy, Cristina, and Cynthia. He had not forgotten me. He had a bottle of beer, which he indicated was for me. He waved briefly, got into his car, and drove away.

Another memorable event was closer to home. It happened when I was preparing for a trip to the Philippines in 1966, my first visit since I left the country for the US in 1954. As a *sarabo* (gift) for father, I would bring him six cans of Hills Brothers' coffee. Since we intended to take the train from Ann Arbor to San Francisco where we were to board the *President Wilson*, I decided to purchase the coffee in that city where the company had one of its main offices.

From the hotel in San Francisco I called the office of the Hills Brothers' Coffee as listed in the Yellow Pages. I carefully asked if I could purchase six small cans of coffee as gift for my father to be delivered directly to the *President Wilson*, which was docked at the San Francisco harbor while loading for the trip to the Philippines.

The secretary that received my original inquiry politely transferred my call from one person to another until I found myself talking to someone who identified himself as one who was in charge of exports for the company! At that point I became a bit apprehensive. I apologized that there might be some misunderstanding for all I wanted, and I repeated carefully, were six small cans of coffee. The man at the other end of the line assured me that there was no misunderstanding. His office, he said, would deliver to the *President Wilson* a box containing six cans of coffee. He added, "Please accept it as a gift from me!" "But I do not understand," I responded, more confused than ever. The man at the other end of the line chuckled, and said, "I was assigned to the Philippines where I lived with my wife and children for a number of years. We remember the happy times we had and how nicely we were treated. Please accept the coffee for your father as a small token of my appreciation of our stay in the Philippines." I cannot overemphasize how touched I was, especially knowing that sometimes tourists going to the Philippines are warned to watch out for pickpockets and other shady characters. I requested his name and address where I sent, as a gift, a case of San Miguel beer.

The smell of hot coffee and freshly baked bread still triggers a memory about the wee hours of a cold morning, parked on a roadside in a quiet neighborhood just outside the border of Lesotho in southern Africa. With four African Americans and a couple from Lesotho, we had traveled in two cars from Swaziland to Lesotho. Starting from Mbabane in Swaziland immediately after dinner, we had driven all night and finally stopped before daybreak in a residential neighborhood just outside Maseru. The man from Lesotho, our guide and also an employee of one of the USAID programs in Swaziland, informed us that the border was closed and would not be open until daylight. "We will sleep and rest in the car for an hour or two," he suggested.

I decided to get out of the car, stretch my legs, and take stock of my surroundings. It was a nice suburban neighborhood of single-family dwellings along a narrow paved road. It was chilly and dark, and I could smell the flowers from the gardens. How peaceful, I thought. Then I detected the unmistakable aroma of freshly baked bread.

I walked slowly for about two blocks following that smell through the dark and quiet neighborhood. Lo and behold, a lighted one-story building, a beehive of activity inside—it was a bakery! I approached the building eagerly and looked in. After the workers noticed me, I inquired if I could buy bread. "Of course," they assured me. They also asked if I wanted coffee. With a long-handled hook, someone pulled a kettle from the cavernous oven and poured some coffee in a cup for me. I told them I had five friends sleeping in the cars two blocks away, and could I have coffee for them, too? They assembled an assortment of cups, and asked one of the workers to help me carry the bread and coffee to the cars. When I paid, they only took money for the bread. The coffee was on the house, they told me.

Needless to say how surprised and pleased I was, but not as surprised as my fellow travelers who grumbled initially when I knocked at the car window to wake them up. But they went after the hot coffee and warm crusty bread with gusto before they finally got around to asking me where I had gotten them! I collected the assorted empty cups, returned them to the bakery, and we resumed our trip to Maseru.

One summer in Cyprus while Judy and I were driving from Nicosia to Paphos, we passed by an improvised lean-to along an isolated stretch of the highway. It was a shade for a watermelon vendor. Since it was noontime and Cyprus was at the time hot and dry, the watermelons looked inviting indeed. I also liked the idea of buying from that vendor, whose stand was just made of sticks with an old blanket and some branches for a roof. I stopped and got out of the car.

An elderly man seated on a wooden bench greeted me warmly. He seemed to be eating his lunch. Seated next to the old man was a little boy probably no more than six years old. I assumed he was the grandson, who had brought grandpa's lunch. I greeted them with the traditional *"Calimera,"* and pointed to the watermelons piled on the ground. He smiled and nodded. But before attending to the sale, he offered his plate to me that had sliced tomatoes, a piece of bread, and a bit of cheese. I nodded approvingly, reached for a sliced tomato, and ate it with gusto. He seemed pleased, and the little boy smiled. Grandpa then selected a nice watermelon for me. I paid him, shook his hand, and thanked him once more. That was good watermelon, and I am sure it was rendered even sweeter by the old man's kind gesture of sharing his simple and healthy lunch.

Because of the hospitality and warmth of the Cypriots, the beauty of the island, and the variety of its cuisine, I always looked forward to my summer assignment in Cyprus. I usually got there about a week before our students arrived at the small residential and private school that Eastern Michigan University rented for lodging and for holding classes for EMU's overseas program. Arriving earlier enabled me to check preparations for the bedrooms, examine the classrooms, review plans for the meals, and look into possible locations for weekend trips. I also prepared a little welcome speech for the first day when all students, usually about thirty, arrived for the courses. But one summer, a day before the planned reception, I lost my voice completely! Not a peep would come out and, needless to say, I was very frustrated. I designated one of the faculty members to give the welcome address.

There was additional and unexpected help. The day following the reception, there was a knock at my door as I was about to take a nap. It was one of the students from Cyprus who apologized for not making an appointment. She brought me a piece of raw ginger for ginger tea, which she said might help my throat. Later that afternoon, as I enjoyed my ginger tea under the lemon trees beside the swimming pool, the elderly gentleman who tended to the garden came over, greeted me, and handed me a plump yellow lemon. He suggested the women in the kitchen could make lemonade for me. "You will get your voice back," he assured me. I was amused and appreciative that my laryngitis had generated such kindness and attention among a variety of people at the school.

The following day, I walked over to the store across the street from the school. It was a place frequented by the students and it carried an assortment of school supplies, cosmetics, and a coffee shop with freshly baked pastries. Before I could even gesture to the friendly storekeeper what I wanted, he rose from his seat with a loud "Aha." He motioned for me to wait, then he poured me a cup of that hot strong coffee that is commonly called "Turkish coffee," though I would never dare call it that in this part of Cyprus which had so recently been partitioned between Greece and Turkey. Before I could attempt to utter my thanks, he said, "Good for your voice!" With all that attention, how could I not get my voice back? In two more days it did indeed return. I was soon busy checking that everything was shipshape for another memorable summer in that enchanting island of Cyprus with its equally beautiful people.

My recollections are full of thoughtfulness and generosity exhibited by strangers during my travels abroad, and remembering them warms my heart. Equally touching is the realization that such unsolicited acts of kindness were extended by people from different stations in life. Given what we hear so much in the news these days about war, need for more transparency in our government, and allegations about corporate greed, these recollections about kind-hearted strangers, often of humble means, strengthen my faith in our capacity to share, to care, and to be kind to one another.

The Old
Neighborhood
in Laoag

After all the adventures of living and working abroad in different countries, which has been exciting and for which I am forever grateful, my tired body and weary mind long for that simple and serene neighborhood in Laoag of yesteryear. It would be a long journey through time to a place probably not known to some of the young Laoaguenos today, and almost forgotten by those whose memories have begun to fade. Fortunately, I remember clearly my old neighborhood where Father's family lived. It was divided into blocks by gravel roads. There were attractive *nipa* huts surrounded by bamboo fences that neatly enclosed a variety of flowering plants. These included *sampaguita, dama de noche, cadena de amor,* yellow bells, canas, and hibiscus. I would never forget the banana plants, *marungay* trees, and *catuday* blossoms. Towering over were the *mansanita, arbor de fuego,* tamarind, mango, and the graceful bamboo.

What a relief to contemplate that simple and quiet neighborhood compared to the noisy and stressful complexity of twenty-first-century suburban America. In that old Laoag neighborhood, a *calesa* (horse carriage), a *carison* (bull cart), or a man on an old bicycle that passed by once in a while was about all the traffic I can remember. And no telemarketers to be sure for there were no telephones in most of the houses. *Siesta* time was serene and quiet, punctuated occasionally by the crow of a rooster or the laughter of children at play.

On weekends when the folks were finally up and about, they tended to their gardens leisurely, the women groomed each other's long shiny hair under the shade of a tree, while some men massaged the bare legs of their fighting roosters and exchanged notes with other *aficionados*. Even then, they were never too busy to engage in a friendly chat with their neighbors. What a contrast to the neighborhood of suburban USA where people seem to be so hurried, whether they are just tending to their yard or going somewhere. An occasional and half-hearted "Hi" is mostly what I remember of many of my American neighbors.

Yes, the simplicity and serenity of that Laoag neighborhood of a long time ago is but a memory now. Sure, recollections are selective, and it probably helps to remember that the common folks had fewer choices in life. They were unaware or less concerned about things like blood pressure, cholesterol, blood sugar, second-hand smoke, sunscreen, antacid, whatever *Viagra* is suppose to do, and so on. Bread for those who could afford it for breakfast or *merienda* (afternoon tea) was just *pan de sal* or *pan de sito*, none of the variety of white, brown, whole wheat, rye, sourdough, sprouted grain, etc. A pair of shoes for those lucky enough was just that, and I do not remember any selections like walking, dancing, jogging, climbing, or running shoes. For the boys, a concession to choice would have been between leather or rubber shoes. I remember how my mother sometimes complimented her friends by exclaiming how "plump" they were for that was surely a sign of good health and prosperity. One of the few pleasures of my *Lola* Sabina Tumaneng Samonte was to smoke several times a day her *dinubla*, tobacco which she rolled herself. Generously proportioned, it was about an inch and a half in diameter and easily ten inches long. She relit it as needed, and the *dinubla* sometimes lasted for a couple of days. I am sure it would not have made any difference to her if we told her what we now know about the relationship between cancer and smoking. To some of the young men smoking was cool, but they would not be caught dead smoking *dinubla*, especially those influenced by Hollywood movies. They smoked American cigarettes that they could purchase by the stick from the *sari sari* store. On a matter of nutrition, I am positive anyone who was foolish enough to suggest that Ilocanos cut down their intake of that heavily salted fish sauce called *boggoong,* for the sake of their health, would have surely taken the risk of being run out of town or worse! Maybe there is something to the saying that "ignorance is bliss." At any rate, that old Laoag neighborhood revives memories of simplicity, serenity, and beautiful gardens with friendly and caring people. It is a restful refuge in the mind for those of us who have strayed far away from home for so long.

Cristina patiently hopes for a bite. Somewhere in England, 1968.

"Look!"

"I am not too sure about this!"

Cindy on a cruise down the Li in Guilin, China, 1984.

Judy feeding lion cubs in South Africa, 1980.

By the Red Sea in Hodeida, North Yemen, 1985.

Cindy, a team leader, the author, and Judy during a trip to Cuba
under the People-to-People Ambassador Program, 2000.

Part V
Epilogue

Diamonds In
The Rough

There must be some truth to the saying that the older we get, the more we recall the past. In my recollections I have revisited people and places of my youth, and also the challenges and the dreams that fueled my determination to move on. But as the shadows of the days grow longer, I like to dwell more on the happy times and, indeed, there were many of them.

One of the consequences of our traditional way of life in Laoag in the 1930s was a population that tended to be rooted in place. There was limited geographic mobility. Sure, there were labor migrations to other parts of the Philippines, even abroad to Hawaii and to the United States. Ilocanos were noted for that. But these tended to be movements of individuals instead of families. Thus, even if there were relatives elsewhere, the families of origin stayed behind. The effect of such a pattern of migration was a relatively stable composition of pupils in the schools. That partly explains why a number of my high school co-graduates had been classmates since kindergarten!

Some members of the generation I grew up with will remember a few of the stories I included in this book. If they were not active participants, at least they were aware of them as part of our culture. Understandably, some of my friends and acquaintances were more daring than others, but I believe we were one in our respect for each other and, on many occasions, in our willingness to share the burden for a common cause. One of the things that stands out in my mind is that, as sophomores in the high school, we initiated a provisional reconstruction of the burned-out high school building.

In 1941 before the invasion of the Philippines by Japan, the Ilocos Norte Provincial High School building was consumed by fire. Because of the war, peoples' priorities were on matters other than investigating the origin of that fire. Thus, I do not think that its cause was ever determined officially. At any rate, the only remaining structure was the concrete shell of a one-story building. When classes resumed in 1946 after the conclusion of the war, the high school building was partially restored with the old galvanized roof and a provisional wooden floor. Classes were held in that building without partitions between the groups. Needless to say, it was not a satisfactory arrangement, but we did the best we could. Our eagerness to get back to school more than made up for a shelter that was nothing more than a roof over our heads.

The sophomore organization, my class, proposed to the principal that he allow the volunteers of our group to work on weekends in setting up partitions between the classes. We explained that the carpentry skills required in constructing the partitions were simple enough, and we could easily provide them. Many of us were either seventeen or eighteen years old and had already taken a course in woodworking that was a requirement in the upper elementary grades. He was pleased, but he wondered how we would pay for materials. We informed him that there were woven bamboo screens that were built as an enclosure around the tennis courts for the town fiesta, and we could probably request the local government to give them to us without cost, since they did not have any more use for them now that the town fiesta was over. Each screen was roughly eight by twelve feet, thus they would be easy to transport and assemble. The principal agreed, but was understandably skeptical. It would have been reasonable for him to wonder, I am sure, if we were taking on something that we could not handle. Or were we going to cause unnecessary disruption to the operation of the school? What if the volunteers sustained injuries?

I volunteered to contact the local government. The local government was so pleased to find some use for the *sawali* walls that they even provided transportation for the materials to the high school grounds. To make a long story short, every weekend volunteers from our sophomore class worked to put up the *sawali* sections, and it was not difficult to do. In a relatively short time, the partitions were installed and classes were soon conducted with some privacy. The noise level was still a problem, but we did not complain.

The improvements were good enough and they stayed that way for a number of years until the school could afford the proper restoration of the school building. How proud we were to see our handiwork. It was not first-class construction work by any means, and those partitions are long gone. But in my mind, they continue to stand as reminders of the cooperation, thoughtfulness, and resourcefulness of a group of young people who grew up during the war.

The passage of time has been kind to us. That same generation that built those provisional partitions in a burned-out high school building went on to join the ranks of responsible citizens. As Teodula S. Andres, our class advisor, wrote for our fiftieth class reunion, "This is the class of 1948 of the Ilocos Norte High School whom I consider to be one of the best classes I have ever had. The members of that class have now reached the age of retirement, and they have served mankind with their utmost ability. I am really proud of the members of the class who have done their best in improving the life of the people in the community in which they lived." We had our share of achievers and leaders in public life in the armed forces, business, education, government, medicine, nursing, science, etc. Remembered with equal admiration were those who quietly assumed their responsibilities as parents and law-abiding citizens. And it was always a source of amusement for me when, during our occasional get-togethers, the women never hesitated to good-naturedly scold our ex-generals or admirals who, for example, might have failed to do a task on time such as mailing invitations for our meetings. In my opinion, one of the achievements I am particularly proud of is that we never allowed rank, power, or wealth to diminish the humility, common touch, and the warm regard we always had for one another.

Class picture in grade three, Laoag Central School.
The author is fifth from the left in the back row, 1938.

Class officers of section one, senior class, with Ms. Teodula S. Andres as class advisor, Ilocos Norte Provincial High School. The author is in the extreme right, front row. 1948.

Judy and the author at a party hosted by co-graduates from
the Ilocos Norte high school, Quezon City, Philippines, 1982.

From L to R: the author, Colonel Daniel Labrado (ret.),
and Commodore Serapio Martillano (ret.). Contemporaries
from elementary grades through high school at a party,
Quezon City, Philippines, 1982.

Some members of Class 1948, Ilocos Norte High School, join the author and Judy for a book launching in Laoag in 2005.
To my left is my niece, Celerina Anama (Quintos). To Judy's right is my Auntie Ilang Reyes who was also a teacher and principal at the high school before her retirement.

"I wonder what kind of debate it would have generated among the teachers and students at our high school if someone suggested that we made him as the mascot of Class 1948!"

Glossary

(The Ilocano translations below are based on the use of the dialect in Laoag, Ilocos Norte. There are variations from one region to another.)

alsong — mortar for pounding rice, made of wood or stone.

aswang — half human and half animal inhabitant of the spirit world.

balayang — banana with large seeds the size of pepper corn.

bangkito — a small wooden stool.

bansag — roofless section of a hut where dishes can be washed and dried.

basar — floor made of bamboo strips.

bogao — paper ribbons attached to the end of a pole for keeping flies away.

bolintik — playing marble.

caldereta — goat stew.

camangaan — where there are mangos (from the root word "manga").

cargadera — carrier mounted over back tire of bicycle.

dwa na-ig — sarong.

galyera — where rooster fighting takes place.

igado — spiced pork loin, liver, and kidney dish.

il-law — kite.

imud — aphrodisiac.

kapri — a black spirit.

kilawen — heavily spiced meat or seafood eaten rare or raw.

linengta — boiled or steamed.

Lola, Lolo — term of reference for grandmother, grandfather.

mang — contraction of manong (masculine) or manang (feminine), a term of respect to a slightly older person.

mangmangkik — a spirit that inhabit the trees.

nipa — palm whose leaves are used for the roof and for walls of huts.

paltat — catfish.

palsi-it — slingshot.

panniki — fruit bat.

pulotan — meat snack usually with a drink.

rama — fish trap made of twigs piled on top of each other.

sinigang — simmered fish or meat with tomatoes, ginger, and other spices.

sipa — a ball woven out of rattan.

sunay — toy top.

tapoy — rice wine.

ticap-ticap — roughly trimmed.

tingol — long hair bundled into a bun.

tinuno — grilled.

References

Corpuz, Onofre, *The Philippines*, Prentice Hall, Inc., 1965.

Francia, Luis, *Eye of the Fish,* Kaya Press, New York, 2001.

Patai, Rafael, *The Arab Mind,* Scribner, 1983.

Punongbayan, Raymundo S., *Legends of the Land*. Kasaysayan, Asia Publishing Company Limited, 1998.

Wurfel, David, *Filipino Politics, Development and Decay*, Cornell University Press, 1988.

Author
and
Illustrator

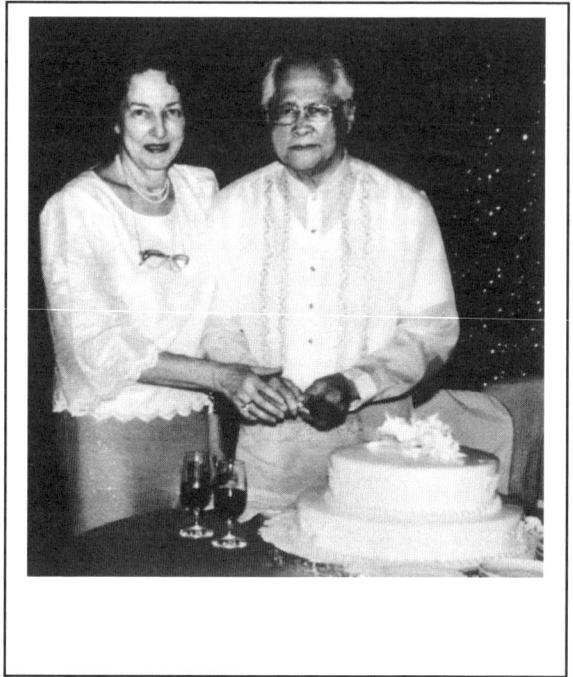

Picture was taken in the Philippines
during the celebration of their
50th wedding anniversary. 2005.

Quirico S. Samonte, Jr., Professor Emeritus, Eastern
Michigan University, and Judith E. Samonte, Research
Associate (retired) of the Institute for Social Research of the
University of Michigan, author and illustrator, respectively,
collaborate again in this book, *Not at the Table, Please!* It is
another collection of entertaining and thoughtful stories about
growing up in the Philippines and about adventures in other
parts of the world.